**Future
Architecture
Platform**

Archifutures

Apocalypse

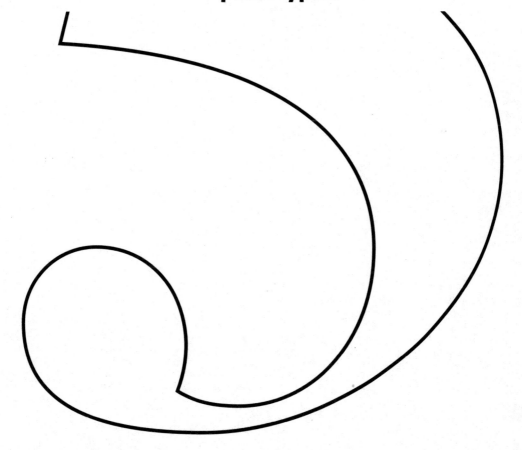

Archifutures

Volume 5: Apocalypse

Future Architecture platform

Archifutures

Volume 5: Apocalypse

A field guide to surviving
the future of architecture

dpr-barcelona   edited by &beyond

Preface

Welcome to *Archifutures Volume 5: Apocalypse*, the fifth part in the ongoing series of field guides to the future of architecture.

Archifutures maps new developments in the fields of contemporary architecture and urban design with contributions from institutions, activists, curators, architects, polemicists, critics and editors involved with the Future Architecture platform. Through conversations and essays, interviews and images, the series lays out an inspiring range of active strategies for the future of the built environment. Both real and imaginary, these are the projects and people shaping tomorrow's architecture and cities.

Archifutures is a publishing project by dpr-barcelona for Future Architecture, a Europe-wide network and EU-funded initiative set up by the Museum of Architecture and Design in Ljubljana, Slovenia in 2015.

Currently available in the *Archifutures* series:

Vol. 1: The Museum – a field guide to communicating the future of architecture

Vol. 2: The Studio – a field guide to speculating upon the future of architecture

Vol. 3: The Site – a field guide to making the future of architecture

Vol. 4: Thresholds – a field guide to navigating the future of architecture

Vol. 5: Apocalypse – a field guide to surviving the future of architecture

The *Archifutures* series is also a pioneering digital and print publishing project. At *archifutures.org* there is an open digital bookshelf and print-on-demand option that allows readers to select texts from the series online, according to individual interest, and order their own custom compilation.

Welcome to the future of architecture.
&beyond
October 2018

Contents

Introduction

This, the fifth volume of *Archifutures* is provocatively titled: *Apocalypse: A field guide to surviving the future of architecture.* In it we are taking the position that the apocalypse is not an imminent event, it is already here – we are experiencing it right now.

We live in challenging times. There is no denying that portents pertaining to the "end of the world", in which we are all threatened by the impending cessation of our existence, are writ large, and that the environmental threats to our planet are overwhelmingly real and extensive. The exclamation "The apocalypse is coming!" is no longer just the preserve of cranks, doomsayers and the pessimistic. However, "the apocalypse" – usually understood as a radical change, after which things will never be the same – is actually an insidious process, not an event. There are communities facing and dealing with apocalypse on a day-to-day basis right now. These communities are resisting, they are adapting, they are surviving as best they can. Despite the implied drama of "apocalypse", the reality is actually far more mundane and surviving it is not about building bunkers, it is about building resilience.

Back in the introduction to Volume 1 of this series, we stated: "The primary objective [of an architect] has to be to improve the environments in which we live without detrimental cost to the environment or our fellow citizens. The commitment of architecture to humanity's needs has to be reaffirmed..." Two years on, as we looked at the hundreds of proposals submitted to the Future Architecture platform's most recent Call for Ideas to select projects around which to centre this book, we were encouraged and excited to see that there are many young architects who clearly subscribe to this point of view and it gave us hope.

The root of the word apocalypse comes from the Ancient Greek *apokálypsis* meaning to uncover, reveal or disclose – which has nothing to do with ending, as most seem to read it. The aim of this volume is to deconstruct and remould the notion of "apocalypse"; to neutralise its drama and to reconsider what it means to live in an age of revelation. What are the futures that these young practitioners aim to reveal? What new prototypical mechanisms of resilience and survival are under construction as we speak? How will they manifest themselves in the built environment?

In many of the projects we looked at, two common threads emerged: 1) a rise in activism and political engagement finding expression through architectural endeavour, and 2) increasingly bold efforts to actively decouple citizens from outmoded political mechanisms and economic structures that no longer reflect the reality of the situation. These young architects are designing systems and structures not just for an apocalyptic present, but also for an expected post-capitalist future. What also became increasingly clear to us was that in the face of an apocalyptic day-to-day reality, when one's world seems to be "ending", hope and trust become radical acts. Many of the projects included here employ these aspects as core strategies, but root them in pragmatism, for example, forms of hope that acknowledge dissent and engage in constant negotiation or forms of trust that embed themselves through dispersed modes of organisation.

Apocalypse: A field guide to surviving the future of architecture opens with the section **Everyday End of the World** and an essay by the Croatian philosopher, author and political activist Srećko Horvat entitled *No Future = No Architecture* in which he argues that for many people the "apocalypse is already here". It provides a lens through which to view the rest of the book and reflects the highly charged and highly polarised environment we are currently living in. Horvat's essay is followed by the contemplative work of Bora Baboci whose visual explorations of spatial belonging reflect another aspect of the mundanity of apocalyptic situations: being stuck, waiting or in transit.

The second section **Adapt and Survive** starts to look at how we could approach some of the problems we are facing and is led by a thought-provoking contemplation on received attitudes to public and private space by Anastassia Smirnova, programme director at the Strelka Institute. In her essay *Manufacturing Solitude: the revelation of loneliness reframed* she talks about how the border between public and private spheres is being actively redrawn and how she responds to that as an architect. In this section too, we find TAB Collective's architectural tools to address and combat right-wing thinking and Maite Borjabad's *Scenographies of Power* project, which takes a critical view of how architecture materialises legal frameworks and political apparatuses through the medium of art and exhibition.

Hope, trust and enthusiasm are perhaps the hardest things to maintain in the face of apocalypse. But they may be our strongest weapons in the battle for survival. The **Radical Hope** section is led by a wonderful project by the Architecture Thinking School For Children in Belarus. The school is founded on the idea – and hope – that extra-curricular education can play a decisive role in a child's future development – with fantastic results. Here too you will find a illuminating and honest conversation between the curators of the Unfolding Pavilion, unofficially part of the 2018 Venice Architecture Biennale, and Space Transcribers discussing their parallel experiences of trying to turn problems into potential when working with the residents of modernist housing estates – themselves radically hopeful projects – in Venice, Italy and Braga, Portugal. Another project here by Symbiocene looks at finding new ways to make use of invasive plant species in polluted and degraded ecosystems, turning competition into cooperation. This section ends with a piece by &beyond's George Kafka on another educational project: the Floating University in Berlin which, for a glorious, but far too long and hot, summer this year, drew people from all over the world to listen, exchange and discuss ideas on a temporary "floating structure inflated with radical hope" in the heart of Berlin.

In the section entitled **Between Consensus and Dissent** we look at how dissent and constant negotiation can be viewed as essential resilience strategies relating to the commons, the local and the post-nation-state. We talk to architectural theorist Stefan Trüby about his headline-making investigations into the physical manifestations of "right-wing spaces" and he reemphasises for us what Srećko Horvat talks about at the beginning: "Autonomous architecture doesn't exist; architecture is always, at the end, or maybe also at the beginning, a political project." Here too Stefan Gruber and Anh-Linh Ngo explain the theoretical foundation behind their excellent new touring exhibition *An Atlas of Commoning* in which they bring politics and confrontation back to the forefront of the architecture agenda. Drawing upon this, they present the historic notion of "sharing" without ownership as a basis for intercultural understanding in their text, *Commoning with a Small c*. These are joined by two very different projects: *The Political Church*, in which Martin Pohl looks at heritage as a tool for engagement in the context of a former church caught in the Balkan conflict, and *If These Walls Could Talk* by the London-based interdisciplinary collective called RESOLVE, who investigated the idea that walls could be used to bring people together, rather than divide them.

Our section called **Progressive Degrowth** contains an illuminating discussion between Matthew Dalziel and Maria Smith, two curators of the 2019 Oslo Architecture Triennale and the originators of two projects from the FA Call for Ideas: METASITU and Tania Tovar Torres. Each initially felt they had completely different understandings of what "degrowth" means in an urban situation, but through their exchange found they had much to share with respect to how to look beyond a present fuelled by unhampered growth. This chapter is joined by a photo essay reflecting an investigation by Tinatin Gurgenidze into the real-life adaptations to the shrinking city condition by residents of the Gladni district of Tblisi in Georgia.

The last section in the book deals with the repercussions and potential of technological empowerment in **Interdependent Individuality**.

Here we find a low-tech architectural tool set for mitigating indoor pollution using the properties of clay by the inspiring Portuguese collective Skrei, an intriguing model for an algorithmic self-organising housing structure by Tomasz Broma, and a proposal by Jason Hilgefort for an Institute of Autonomous Urbanism based on infrastructural "hacks" practiced in Shenzen. In *Power to the Peer*, &beyond editors George Kafka and Fiona Shipwright also engaged the creators of two related projects by DOMA and Phi in a Slack conversation about the distribution of energy and housing via blockchain-based platforms. Both groups are interested in the exploring potential of blockchain systems for the built environment and work at the intersection of peer-to-peer technologies, energy futures and speculative design. We are really looking forward to revisiting these projects in the coming years, along with many of the others mentioned above in the hope that they will be picked up and expanded upon: helping to empower communities worldwide to help themselves build a more resilient future.

On a final note, we have divided this book into sections less for the sake of categorisation and more for the sake of communication and propagation. They are not chapter headings as much as they are further calls for change and action – illustrated by the projects, interviews, dialogues and essays. Just as architects and planners mediate the built environment, so too do editors mediate spaces for the dissemination of information. Our job is to communicate, to make clear, to "reveal". And in challenging times such as these we too need to respond in a proactive way to the apocalyptic present – with hope. So we openly invite any and all to take these seven headings and statements and share them, work with them, improve them, and above all use them to help build a better future for all of us.

George Kafka, Sophie Lovell and Fiona Shipwright,
&beyond

Our Future

The apocalypse is typically understood as a radical moment of change, after which things will never be the same.

This is the moment to rethink the complicity of architecture in the construction of the current state of affairs and to work towards the development of complex and inclusive futures.

&beyond would like to thank all the *Archifutures Volume 5*
contributors, interlocutors and provocateurs, most especially:
Bora Baboci, Maite Borjabad, Tomasz Broma, Eduardo Cassina,
Trajna Collective, Matthew Dalziel, DOMA, Liva Dudareva, Sara
Favargiotti, Davide Tommaso Ferrando, Lena Giovanazzi, Tinatin
Gurgenidze, Jason Hilgefort, Elena Karpilova, Anh-Linh Ngo,
Alexander Novikov, Phi, Martin Pohl, RESOLVE, Skrei, Anastassia
Smirnova, Maria Smith, Space Transcribers, TAB Collective, Tania
Tovar Torres and Stephan Trüby; Ethel Baraona Pohl and César
Reyes Nájera; Matevz Čelik and the whole MAO team.

Our thanks also to everyone who has assisted in mapping out the
architectural beyond for this volume: Fernando Abellanas, Markus
Bader, Anna Fixsen, Benjamin Foerster-Baldenius and Rosario Talevi.

&beyond
October 2018

About &beyond

Founded in Berlin in 2016, &beyond is a transdisciplinary publishing collective of editors, writers and graphic designers. For &beyond, print and digital are not mutually exclusive; simply two aspects of the collective's mission: to communicate things worth saying in a manner worth reading in the age of entanglement.

andbeyond.xyz   @andbeyondxyz

About dpr-barcelona

dpr-barcelona is an architectural research practice based in Barcelona and working within three main areas of interest: publishing, criticism and curating. Their work explores how architecture as a discipline reacts at the intersection between politics, technology, economics and social issues. dpr-barcelona has been a member of the Future Architecture platform since 2016.

dpr-barcelona.com   @dpr_barcelona

Archifutures
Volume 5: Apocalypse
A field guide to surviving the future of architecture
archifutures.org

A publishing project accompanying the Future Architecture platform
futurearchitectureplatform.org

Future Architecture platform is coordinated by
the Museum of Architecture and Design (MAO), Ljubljana
Director Matevž Čelik

Publishing platform concept
dpr-barcelona

Series concept, editing and design
&beyond

Editors Sophie Lovell, Fiona Shipwright, George Kafka, Rob Wilson
and Florian Heilmeyer
Volume 5 editors Sophie Lovell, Fiona Shipwright and George Kafka
Design Diana Portela

andbeyond.xyz

First published in 2018
dpr-barcelona
Viladomat 59 4° 4ª
08015 Barcelona

dpr-barcelona.com

This book is set in Ergilo, Freight Display, Paul Grotesk and Space Mono.
It is printed on Munken Cream 80g paper/Card Graphics 275g. Generated with Print
on Demand Technology

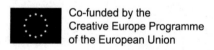

Co-funded by the
Creative Europe Programme
of the European Union

The European Commission support for the production of this publication does not
constitute an endorsement of the contents which reflects the views only of the authors,
and the Commission cannot be held responsible for any use which may be made of the
information contained therein.

Printed in Spain
Legal Deposit: B 26540-2018
ISBN: 978-84-949388-1-8

Everyday End of the World

Climate change, resource shortages and mass migration: for millions around the world living under apocalyptic conditions is an everyday reality. We all need to recognise that fact and adapt our thinking accordingly.

No
Future

=

No
Architecture

By Srećko Horvat
Illustrations by Janar Siniloo

**Using architecture theory
to think about our common future**

No Future = No Architecture

Using architecture theory to think about our common future

By Srećko Horvat
Illustrations by Janar Siniloo

"The responsibility for architects today is not just to be reactive but also to construct a different future."

The Croatian philospher Srećko Horvat was invited to give one of the opening lectures of the Future Architecture 2018 Creative Exchange conference at the MAO in Ljubljana. This essay is an adaptation of that lecture and provides a fitting opening to set the theme of this volume of Archifutures.

We are living in an era in which there is a certain pre-apocalyptic feeling floating around. We are bombarded daily by scenes of new walls or borders, detention camps and boats full of refugees, climate change and the possibility of a nuclear war. Our reality increasingly resembles. Alfonso Cuarón's film *Children of Men*, for example, depicted a world where refugees are in cages in the centres of Western cities and acts of terrorism occur every week. If we look at Europe today, we can see an increasing retreat towards a dangerous concept of sovereignty. Other dystopian scenarios of how the world might end include the growing effects of climate change. On top of this increasing pre-apocalyptic narrative, we also have the very real possibility that a crazy guy with orange hair could post a tweet and provoke a nuclear war. So, on the one hand, we are dealing with a narrative that is trying to create an atmosphere of fear, but on the other, we are facing something much more dangerous, namely that this narrative is becoming inscribed into our reality, which means that today we are genuinely facing an apocalypse.

On the January 13, 2018 at 8:07 a.m. the people of Hawaii woke up to the following message: "Emergency Alert: BALLISTIC MISSILE THREAT INBOUND TO HAWAII. SEEK IMMEDIATE SHELTER. THIS IS NOT A DRILL". I happened to be in Belgrade at the time. It was almost evening and Serbians were getting ready to celebrate the Orthodox New Year. This is the reality we live in today:

Srećko Horvat

Srećko Horvat (b. 1983) is a Croatian philosopher, author and political activist. He has published widely in Croatian, German, English and French. He is the author of *What Does Europe Want? The Union and its Discontents* (with Slavoj Žižek) and The Radicality of Love. He was also involved in setting up the Democracy in Europe Movement 2025 (DiEM 2025) along with Yanis Varoufakis.

in one corner of the world people wake up thinking they have 15 minutes until the end of the world and in another people are celebrating New Year's Eve.

The Hollywood actor Jim Carey commented on the experience on his Twitter account: "I woke up this morning in Hawaii with ten minutes to live. It was a false alarm, but a real psychic warning. If we allow this one-man Gomorrah and his corrupt Republican congress to continue alienating the world we are headed for suffering beyond all imagination. ;^\".[1] Others at that time had different reactions. A guy called Joshua Keoki Versola was home alone, and he decided that the best thing to do was open an expensive bottle of Japanese Hibiki 21 whisky. He said: "I was about to start pouring drinks and go out in style", adding: "What are we going to do in this situation? We really can't do anything but just try and make the best of it."[2] What should we do? It is a good question. It took 38 minutes (an eternity for anybody living through such a situation) for the authorities in Hawaii to send a new message saying that this was in fact a drill. They said: "It was a mistake made during a standard procedure at the change of a shift and an employee pushed the wrong button."[3]

At the same time as all this was happening, the CIA, who are supposed to know about and be tracking nuclear threats, published something on Twitter about pandas while President Trump was playing golf. Maybe the reason the world did not end up in a nuclear war on January 13, 2018 has less to do with the Cold War logic of MAD (mutual assured destruction) but far more to do with contingency. If the CIA had not been obsessed with panda diplomacy and if Donald Trump had not been playing golf, maybe somebody would have pushed the "right" button. Or, even if they had done nothing, what if Kim Jong-un

1 twitter.com/jimcarrey/ status/95228449425 7508352?lang=en (accessed August 16, 2018)

2 "Hawaii ballistic missile false alarm results in panic", Julia Carrie Wong and Liz Barney, *The Guardian*, January 14, 2018. theguardian.com/ us-news/2018/jan/13/ hawaii-ballistic-missile- threat-alert-false-alarm (accessed August 16, 2018)

3 "Missile threat alert for Hawaii a false alarm; officials blame employee who pushed 'wrong button'", Zachary Cohen, *CNN*, January 13, 2018. edition.cnn.com/ 2018/01/13/politics/hawaii- missile-threat-false-alarm/ index.html (accessed August 16, 2018)

in North Korea had believed that the alarm was real and pushed the actual button? In either case the people in Hawaii or the people celebrating New Year's Eve in Serbia would not have survived the day.

The point of this introduction is to show that the apocalypse could happen anywhere and at any time. If it happens in Hawaii today, it will probably also happen in Slovenia or in any other part of the world.

Just a few days after Trump became President of the United States, on January 20, 2017, *The New Yorker* published an article entitled "Doomsday Prep for the Super-Rich".[4] On the one hand, we have what psychoanalysts would call "fetishist disavowal", or denial, which means that we know

4 "Doomsday Prep for the Super-Rich", Evan Osnos, *The New Yorker*, January 30, 2017. newyorker.com/magazine/2017/01/30/doomsday-prep-for-the-super-rich (accessed August 16, 2018)

"This is not a joke anymore, this is mainstream."

the apocalypse is happening but we still keep driving our big cars and polluting the world. But on the other, and which this article illustrated nicely, we also have a sense of acceptance of the apocalypse. And something more than acceptance; the super-rich are even preparing for it. For instance, according to the same article the CEO of Reddit, Steve Huffman, even went through laser eye surgery because: "If the world ends – and not even if the world ends, but if we have trouble – getting contacts or glasses is going to be a huge pain in the ass." He later adds that he is prepared for the aftermath and event of "the temporary collapse of our government and structures... I own a couple of motorcycles. I have a bunch of guns and ammo. Food. I figure that, with that, I can hole up in my house for some amount of time." The article goes on to explain that García Martínez, author of the book *Chaos Monkeys*, "bought five wooded acres on an island in the Pacific Northwest". Other examples include Peter Thiel, one of Facebook's first investors, a Trump supporter and CEO of Palantir, which deals with big data. He was one of the first of this group to get New Zealand citizenship. In the first 48 hours after Trump's election, the New Zealand immigration website had a 2,500 percent increase in traffic.[5] This is not a joke anymore, this is mainstream.

5 "Why Silicon Valley billionaires are prepping for the apocalypse in New Zealand", Mark O'Connell, *The Guardian*, February 15, 2018. theguardian.com/ technology/2017/jan/29/ silicon-valley-new-zealand-apocalypse-escape (accessed August 16, 2018)

Another article published by CNN presents photographs of billionaires' apocalypse-proof luxury bunkers.[6] And in an even more interesting article, *Forbes* magazine has commissioned maps projecting how the post-apocalyptic

6 "Billionaire bunkers: How the 1% are preparing for the apocalypse", Elizabeth Stamp, *CNN*, October 17, 2017. edition.cnn.com/style/article/ doomsday-luxury-bunkers/ index.html (accessed August 16, 2018)

7 "The Shocking Doomsday
Maps Of The World And The
Billionaire Escape Plans",
Jim Dobson, *Forbes*, June
10, 2017. forbes.com/sites/
jimdobson/2017/06/10/
the-shocking-doomsday-
maps-of-the-world-and-the-
billionaire-escape-plans/
#22e4acdf4047 (accessed
August 16, 2018)

"What if the apocalypse has actually already happened?"

8 "Trump's border wall
through the eyes of
an architecture critic",
Christopher Hawthorne,
Los Angeles Times, January 4,
2018. scribd.com/article/
368426029/Trump-s-Border
-Wall-Through-The-Eyes-
Of-An-Architecture-Critic
(accessed August 16, 2018)

world will look in a rapid climate change situation. [7] It describes how wealthy individuals are buying up millions of acres of land in "dry territories in the United States such as Montana, New Mexico, Wyoming and Texas". This is the reality: a pre- or post-apocalyptic narrative and the super-rich preparing for it. Or another example: the aforementioned Thiel was the one who developed and invested in the idea of a floating city called "Seastead", reminiscent the 1995 post-apocalyptic Kevin Costner movie *Waterworld* that had precisely the same scenario, namely that water levels will rise and people like Thiel will build these kinds of libertarian utopias to live in.

The point of all these dystopian examples is not to scare you into believing that the apocalypse is coming – although it probably is. The point is to deconstruct this particular apocalyptic narrative. What if the apocalypse has actually already happened? In the sense that it has already happened for the majority of people in the world. The fact that the super-rich or many others have not yet experienced this kind of apocalyptic situation doesn't mean that it has not already taken place in Somalia, in Bangladesh or at the border between Mexico and the US.

So what responsibility does architecture and urbanism have in this? An article published in the *Los Angeles Times* by the architecture critic Christopher Hawthorne compares eight prototypes for Trump's wall to the work of Peter Zumthor and calls it a kind of "accidental minimalism". [8] The projected length of this wall is around 2,000 miles but today nearly 700 miles of the border are already covered by walls and fences. Again, the apocalypse has already happened for someone trying to make their way from Mexico to the United States. And it is the responsibility of the architect to design this apocalypse.

Another way that the apocalypse and architecture are connected concerns what happens to buildings during earthquakes. It opens up an interesting discussion about the critique of ideology because the dystopian images of collapsed buildings in the tragic events you see from Puerto Rico, Haiti and Taiwan, for example, are presented as "natural disasters", i.e. it is just something that happens and we humans do not have the capability to prevent it. But if we learned anything from Walter Benjamin, who was writing about it in the early twentieth century, or Roland Barthes in the mid-twentieth, something that is an historic political event. Peter Hallward, who is an inspiring philosopher, not an architect, said, for example, that the results of the 2010 earthquake in Haiti were not a natural catastrophe, but resulted from bad planning and bad infrastructure and affected mainly people from a specific class origin – the underdogs.

The June 2017 fire in the Grenfell Tower in London, in which 72 people lost their lives, is another clear example of the connection between class origin, bad politics and also, in a way, architecture. This residential tower block was situated in Kensington and Chelsea. Anyone who has been to London knows that Kensington and Chelsea is a borough where you can see all the contradictions of global capitalism in a very small area. Why did the Grenfell Tower fire happen? It happened because the super rich don't really care about those that don't have money. According to some data, the mean income in Kensington and Chelsea is 158,000 GBP [9] – the highest in the UK, which is still not enough to buy a home in the area with an average house price of 1.5 million GBP. The result is that this tower, whose condition points back to Margaret Thatcher and austerity politics, was effectively just left to burn. Even in a luxurious neighbourhood in the middle

9 "Do you earn more or less than the average for your borough?", Sam Brodbeck, *The Telegraph*, May 3, 2017. telegraph.co.uk/money/consumer-affairs/do-earn-less-average-borough/ (accessed September 3, 2018)

of a modern metropolis like London, the apocalypse is happening somewhere for someone.

There has always been a debate about whether architecture is political or not. Since Vitruvius there has been a tradition of saying architecture is never political, but that it has been used to pacify populations and avoid conflict, which is, to a certain degree, true. According to tradition, the role of the architect is to negotiate between different interests, which is also, to a certain extent, true. So basically the architect is a figure of consensus, rather than conflict. Then of course there is the famous Le Corbusier quote; "architecture or revolution", which forces us to choose between architecture and social change. If you move forward to 1994, just two years after Francis Fukuyama's *End of History and the Last Man*, Bernard Tschumi's book *Architecture and Disjunction* was published, which does not have an "or" in the title, but an "and". In the book Tschumi (influenced by the situationists Guy Debord and Jacques Derrida) shows that architecture is always political. He even says that sometimes you have to commit a murder in order to appreciate architecture, or sometimes you have to have sex on a street in order to understand what kind of urbanism or architecture exists there. [10] It is enough to remember the role Baron Haussman played in in the design of Paris because the authorities wanted to stop the revolution by building very wide boulevards so the people could not build barricades – and it functioned to a certain degree. Then, of course, there is the most famous example from the twentieth century, the role of Albert Speer. His designs for Berlin and Germania showed clearly that architecture is not only connected to politics, in this case to Adolf Hitler, but that architecture actually produces social change – in this case, dystopian social change, namely: totalitarianism. The most recent examples are Trump's wall or the Grenfell disaster.

10 See Bernard Tschumi, *Architecture and Disjunction,* MIT Press, 1994

This all brings us to the place where we are today. I was really intrigued by the initiative of this pan-European Future Architecture platform, not only because I too am part of a pan-European movement fighting for democracy at a European level along the lines of the idea that you cannot fight the current climate, energy and economic crisis at the level of the nation state. To quote Matevž Čelik, director of the Future Architecture platform:

"The architecture of the future will not only be a practice that necessarily leads just to the construction of buildings and artefacts, but will also lead us to new fields in which to operate."

I think this is a highly important point since architects today are increasingly becoming slaves of big investors or autocratic regimes. They have to build what they have to build, but this does not annul their responsibilities. Maybe

I am being naïve, because I do not come from this field, but I think the situation has started to change. If the NSA, CIA, Palantir, Facebook and the like are making a topology of our own lives, let us make a topology about them. Let's leak some documents, let's make a topology of the "architecture" they are constructing and the kind of dystopian futures they are imagining. I think there has been a trend recently – and I hope it is more than a trend – for architects to focus more on this question. However, the responsibility for architects today is not just to be reactive but also to construct a different future. Let us not react to the refugee crisis by saying let's be smart like IKEA and design new homes for them. Let's try to act ahead in a way that will make a future with refugees, new walls and new wars, climate change and ecological disasters impossible. Even if it is not yet the end of the world, architects have the power and responsibility for building a different future. Because if there is no future, there is no architecture. ■

Idles

Apocalyptic observations
on spatial belonging

By Bora Baboci

The *Idles* series of images is inspired by fundamental constructive elements; walls, gates, borders, columns, erosion, thresholds, surfaces. However, given their incomplete nature, they remain spatial proposals that don't yet represent anything in particular. Apocalyptic and abstract, the images respond to the shockwaves that global migration and virtual realities are giving to spatial disciplines. They try to expose the ambiguous place that typology holds in our shifting spatial language and the questions this has raised about our capacity to spatially belong.

During migration time at Tempelhof I observed flocks of birds on their resting grounds just in front of the refugee camp. Here the tragedy of war and the annual migration for seasonal survival are both embodied in the displacement of two species in a shared landscape that was, curiously enough, a former airport field. The observation triggered further reflection on the physical and psychological experience of displacement as well as the spaces where people rest between two journeys. It then became a video piece called *Prayer Between Journeys.* It also triggered the necessity to read this landscape as a place of waiting and protection, a sanctuary rather than the field of an abandoned airport, an extensive space for the imagination to project multiple and overlapping landscapes.

Another research project, on the mosques built within the Berlin city block system, suggests that the way the faithful use the interior of the blocks to access the temple is similar to the procession they would usually follow within the spatial arrangement of a typological mosque. The interior of the Berlin block becomes the *temenos*, the ground surrounding or adjacent to a religious temple,

Bora Baboci

Bora Baboci (Albania, 1988) lives between Tirana and Berlin. She studied architectural design and criticism at the University of Toronto, Universidad Torcuato di Tella in Buenos Aires and holds a master's degree from the Universitat Politecnica de Catalunya. From 2015 she worked as researcher at the Technische Universität Berlin, focusing on experimental housing and public typologies in the context of global migration. Since 2017 she has been working towards a more independent and experimental practice.

Opposite: Detail from the *Idles* series, photography, 2017. Image: Bora Baboci

Erosion Net, Areal series, pencil and white guache on cardboard (2017). Image: Bora Baboci

and the faithful adapt their behaviours relative to their spatial remembrance. The sensation is still produced though the typology of the building that is not present.

Video still from *Prayer Between Journeys* (2017). Image: Bora Baboci

As the site *par excellence* of the human being, the body stores empathy, imagination, spatial behaviour and

intuition. It holds a gestural inheritance that can be
projected onto a given space and appropriated with
subjective narratives, which, when shared, allow for
a collective space to emerge. Space has this quality;
it triggers an intuitive response that doesn't necessarily
need to be mediated by discourse. Thus a former airport
field can be perceived as a sanctuary, the interior of a
Berlin block can be walked through as a temenos and
the abandoned foundations of a construction site can be
perceived as a temple.

In the actual condition of wanderers, such as refugees,
tourists and, the perpetually non-settling urban youth,
this capacity to appropriate may be essential in coping
with displacement. However, without the *appropriate*
conditions, doing away with the site may result in a
psychologically painful experience. With this in mind,
Idles looks beyond the gaze of the beholder towards
overlaps where the co-existence of unrelated systems of
meaning and spatial associations thrive. In doing so, it
hopes to recognise the spatial conditions that facilitate
these overlaps, as one way of coping with some of the
anxiety produced by ongoing displacement. ■

Adapt and Survive

The reality of the apocalyptic condition is quite mundane. Surviving it is not about building bunkers, it is about changing our approach and building resilience in an everyday way.

Manufacturing Solitude

The revelation of loneliness reframed

By Anastassia Smirnova

Manufacturing Solitude

The revelation of loneliness reframed

By Anastassia Smirnova

"Most design efforts are aimed at combating loneliness through the creation of communal and shared spaces, rather than through improvement of quality in the experience of being alone."

Anastassia Smirnova, programme director at the Strelka Institute, co-founder of the SVESMI architecture office and member of the Future Architecture platform Advisory Board, looks at the very personal everyday apocalypse of loneliness and wonders about another human need: that of solitude. She suggests there is much to be learned from taking a different approach to both.

All solitude is selfish. No one now
Believes the hermit with his gown and dish
Talking to God (who's gone, too); the big wish
Is to have people nice to you, which means
Doing it back somehow.
Virtue is social...

Philip Larkin

In 2017, the United Kingdom officially acknowledged that loneliness has become a national problem. Rachel Reeves, co-chair of the Jo Cox Commission on Loneliness appointed to research the issue, stated that "in the last few decades, loneliness has escalated from personal misfortune into a social epidemic." Recent surveys have revealed that indeed many Britons from a range of age groups and incomes are feeling lonely both at home and at work, which leads to multiple societal challenges and even damages the economy to the tune of 32 billion GBP per year, according to government figures. In January 2018, Prime Minister Theresa May even appointed a new Minister for Loneliness. The Jo Cox Commission remains active, showing determination to combat this "giant evil" and encouraging public discussion and recognition of the dire consequences of this crisis.

Anastassia Smirnova

Anastassia Smirnova is a writer and researcher who has worked as a playwright, journalist and author of the Russian *Afisha Guide Book to Amsterdam.* She lives in the Netherlands where, together with Alexander Sverdlov, she founded SVESMI, the first Dutch-Russian office for architecture, urbanism and multidisciplinary research. She is also a member of the Future Architecture platform Advisory Board.

"Giant Evil"

Previous spread: House of Text lonely visitor. Image: SVESMI

By comparison, other Western countries seem to be less concerned with the isolation of their citizens or, at least, do not recognise the problem as being of particular importance. However, the idea that the neoliberalist world order in general is disconnecting, disengaging and isolating humans from each other, is one that continues to resurface. Critics of free market capitalism often link the inequality and competition that this political and economic system generates, with the growing numbers of disillusioned and lonely individuals.

Whether neoliberalism is indeed inherently destructive at an individual level or not, there are certain modern tendencies – such as increased mobility and the proliferation of social media – that, despite many positive effects, also weaken traditional social ties and prompt further atomisation of human hives. The prospect of our promised automated future with its proliferation of machines replacing humans is not much brighter. The bliss of singularity may make the world a better-connected place, but it will probably make it a very lonely one too.

Houses for Being Alone

Contemporary designers and architects have their ways of addressing this issue. We usually feel obliged to design socially engaging spaces. For any project today, no matter what the programme of the building is, it is almost obligatory to spell out "openness", "community feel", and "shared services". It is a mantra that seems to guarantee public recognition and buy-in into a developer's plan. More and more people in all stages of the lifecycle feel lonely, we are told, but most of the design efforts are aimed at combating loneliness through the creation of communal and shared spaces, rather than through improvement of quality in the very experience of being alone.

Is it possible to turn loneliness into productive solitude through spatial organisation and programming? Could architects do anything about this "giant evil" apart from offering projects of optimistic collectivism and communal rhetoric? These questions are not easy to answer. Architects do not often voluntarily design for solitude and isolation – unless they get a commission for a high security facility. It seems too risky, too irresponsible towards society and also too insignificant a task in the greater scheme of things. How many great modern spaces for being alone can one name? Louis Barragan's own house, which he turned into an eremitic architectural lab; Le Corbusier's *Cabanon*; Marcel Breuer's designs for monastic cells at the St. John's Abbey in Minnesota... To be honest, not many examples spring to mind.

Others, for instance Ryue Nishizawa's seminal Moriyama House – a collection of cube-rooms commissioned by a lonely music connoisseur – are usually accompanied by defensive narratives. The authors, and even their most devoted commentators, feel obliged to rehabilitate such endeavours. Thus, the famous documentary *Moriyama-San* by Ila Bêka and Louise Lemoine (2005) tells the story of Mr. Moriyama's retreat in the centre of Tokyo in a way that attempts to prove that it is not what it seems: the owner is not a true urban recluse after all (there are tenants in his distributed house) and the house itself is better integrated into the neighbourhood (people know who lives there) than the project images suggest.

The Israeli-French artist and sculptor Absalon is probably the most inquisitive creative mind of the last decades who has vigorously and consistently experimented with spaces for solitude. In 1992, he completed a whole set of measurements corresponding to everyday routines –

> **"Is it possible to turn loneliness into productive solitude through spatial organisation and programming?"**

eating, sleeping, working, washing, etc. – and, in 1993, began building a collection of individual cells for solitary living in Tokyo, New York, Tel Aviv, Paris, Zurich and Frankfurt. With this project he challenged the prevailing discourse of community-oriented urban life. His so-called *Cellules* are currently on display in various art museums, often described in his own words as "bastions of resistance against a society that prevents me from becoming what I must become".

It is, of course, easy to brand Absalon as a stray rebel and his efforts marginal: he always readily acknowledged that he designed the cells only for himself, no matter how prototypical they were. But what has been explained by museum professionals as a unique artistic experience could perhaps become an important part of every primary school programme – each individual from a very young age probably should search for his or her own formula for a productive space for being alone.

Even an architect who claims to be independent from universal trends and interested only in the very core issues of architectural profession, Peter Zumthor, has taken rather an evasive stance on spaces for solitary existence. His Bruder Klaus Field Chapel (2007) in Germany is a tiny sanctum/monastic cell in the middle of a field that was in fact designed for no dweller at all. It is a privately-commissioned symbolic monument to a fifteenth century hermit, who is also a patron saint of Switzerland and whose *real* cell and chapel still exist near Lucerne.

A small-scale mecca for architectural students and a handful of catholic nomads, the Field Chapel may be offering solace, but it only prompts you to marvel – for the duration of the visit – at how productive spiritual isolation

"Each individual from a very young age probably should search for his or her own formula for a productive space for being alone. "

could have been in the past. It tells almost nothing about what its contemporary equivalent could be and for what purpose it could have been created today. Paradoxically enough, since it is a publicly accessible monument to a historical figure, the very purpose of the place is to attract visitors; therefore, the better it works, the less chance you have to be left alone there.

In countries, such as Russia, that are very slowly recovering from the trauma of forced collectivism and whose citizens are enjoying their very relative privacy after decades of surviving under the eye of Big Brother, *living alone* – on your own – has always been considered an utmost luxury. Even during the time of feverish construction of mass housing under Khrushchev's rule, when thousands of families finally got out of barracks and *communalkas* and into their own homes, apartments for one remained in huge deficit. For socialist planners, people interested in living alone were, by definition, pariahs.

Public / Private

Apart from much esteemed trips out to "nature", the only true possibilities for productive solitary moments in urban Soviet Russia were offered by public spaces such as museums and libraries. Despite being mostly pretty

Libraries always provided the high-quality solitude in public. Dostoyevsky Library in Moscow at night. Project by SVESMI. Image: Frans Parthesius

crowded, these institutions helped to create a bubble of anonymity around each visitor, allowing for the focused privacy in silence that citizens were deprived of elsewhere. For the generations of students and researchers who grew up under non-democratic regimes, a table for one with a lamp at the public library remained a spatial formula of individual freedom and a strong cultural meme.

"You feel lonely because you were never taught how to be without others."

In our overly-busy world, the border between public and private spheres (and between public and private space) is being actively redrawn. Today, public space accommodates more and more activities that used to be understood as purely domestic. We tend to dwell publicly, opening up our private realm to all kinds of external intrusions; we constantly share things, images, thoughts, spaces, services, etc. with others. How does all this openness correspond to growing numbers of lonely humans, especially young people? Is there a correlation at all? Can we maybe assume that this merging of public and private domains – albeit voluntary – has some of the effects that collective existence once had on the citizens of Communist countries? You feel lonely, because you are never properly alone. You feel lonely because you were never taught how to be without others - disconnected and isolated - and still be well, be productive, at least, for a period of time. And this seems to be something one needs to learn.

This kind of reasoning seems relevant and actual to the work my office SVESMI has been doing for the last two years in Moscow for the Pushkin Museum of Fine Arts. Like many large-scale museums in big cities, the Pushkin Museum is expanding, acquiring adjacent buildings and adding more and more space to the enfilades of its existing rooms. Our team was commissioned to redesign one of these new additions, a bourgeois apartment block built in 1914 by a family of rich merchants in tune with the trends of Vienna and Berlin at the time. We were tasked with an almost impossible assignment: to transform this historical monument - a collection of former private rooms and corridors - into a contemporary museum, the so-called House of Text. Without being able to move or demolish a single wall or to alter a layout, we still had to create a space for an ever-changing trove of extremely diverse exhibits related to textual materials - books, magazines, manuscripts, scrolls, documents, etc. Although, we already had broad experience in designing public libraries, this "meta-library" presented a unique challenge. We had to turn the building, initially designed as purely private and domestic (with all its infrastructural and spatial limitations), into a public cultural institution. All transformations were to be done only by the means of light and furniture arrangements and through the introduction of new protocols of use and restoration.

In response to this brief, we proposed to see all the apparently negative characteristics of the building as positive, recognising and emphasising the value of a

House of Text:
A Room with a View

House of Text is a museum that exploits the original structure of the bourgeois apartment block and remains a collection of private rooms – former bedrooms, living rooms, reading rooms, etc. Enfilade. Image: SVESMI

(private) room even within a public realm. In contrast to other museums, which measure their success by the number of visitors per year, the House of Text introduces another logic: it is a slow space for lonely visitors, allowing for time being spent with the exhibits in different ways, by working, reading, meditating or simply looking out of a window. A painting-like image of a person sitting at the table, lit with the natural light – both at home and away from home – became very central to the project. We tried to imagine a democratic public place capable of distilling a very personal, solitary experience and offering the level of concentration, which would be very hard to achieve in a private space so exposed and overly connected today. This museum, which has no permanent collection and is envisaged as a container for many temporary shows, should establish a special connection between a visitor and an exhibit: that of a focused and unrushed exchange.

The House of Text is still in the making; the new museum will not open its rooms to the public until 2021. A huge task ahead is to sequence our concept with multiple curatorial schemes, creating a space with quite a nuanced agenda, which, at the same time, will remain flexible and able to accommodate a variety of narratives. We are also developing a diversity of scenarios for visiting for a wide range of users. So the challenge is: how to make this private/public experience productive for all? How to distribute exhibits across rooms? How to ensure the privacy of the individual without jeopardising the publicness of this cultural institution in the centre of the

The entrance zone is designed as a place for individual planning of the museum trajectory. No lines and no rush: the museum consultant will help you to find the right room for your solitary experience. Reception. Image: SVESMI

European metropolis? Almost every one of the six hundred rooms in this museum will have its own particular setting. Depending on its size, position in the building, levels of noise and insolation, the quality of its historical interior, the view from it onto the city and many other characteristics, each room will offer a different degree and quality of solitude. Theoretically at least, there will be a chance for everyone to find his or her perfect space in this house. ■

Architecture vs. Politics

A critique of political agendas with architectural elements

By TAB Collective

Architecture should take a role in criticising political habits that influence the built environment and social life. Politics and architecture have a close relationship. It is politics that influences architecture and urbanism; laws, funding and competitions for public projects – all of these determine the architectural process. So what role can architects play in reconfiguring political agendas? We are currently experiencing a global rise in populism and nationalism in parallel with an ever-growing displacement of people from their homes, which challenge the status of nationhood. What tools can we use to combat old ideas that are starting to dominate once again in Europe and elsewhere?

Despite our diverse backgrounds, we, the members of TAB, consider ourselves to be Europeans, based in Vienna. Austria's history is tied up with nationalism, right-wing thinking and separation. Unfortunately, it is not only our past, but also our present that seems to be affected by it. We have devised a range of architectural tools to address and combat this kind of thinking, three examples of which are outlined below.

One architectural project we worked on concerned embassies. We asked ourselves: what does an embassy stand for? What is its task? What does an embassy mean to us? In German, the word "embassy" (*Botschaft*) also means "message". So, we turned away from considering an embassy as an architectural building and started to create a concept that aims to spread a transboundary message to a crumbling Europe.

We wanted to bring back and embed the original "Idea of Europe", one of togetherness, so we came up with a scenario for a possible future called *The Golden Age of Nothing*. It is a dystopian story book about Europe set in the near future.

TAB Collective

TAB is a think tank based in Vienna, Austria. They focus on socio-political topics in connection with architecture and design. In their theoretical and architectural projects, they aim to question current agendas and strive for different solutions. The collective's contributors are Philippe Jans, Therese Leick, Charles Rauchs and Wilhelm Scheruebl.

The Golden Age of Nothing

Opposite: Recollect Space.
Image: TAB Collective

It tells, in words and pictures, of separated states where nationalism, segregation and fear of the unknown have taken over our societies. Each of the 19 chapters is told by a character and resident who is trapped in one of the newly created states. These stories were then translated into over 20 different European languages in order to create a Europe-wide network – one that transcends borders and exemplifies the idea of a united Europe.

A distopian scenario,
The Golden Age of Nothing.
Image: TAB Collective

Recollect Space

Recollect Space is a project in which architecture is the reflection of a story. We wanted to raise awareness about the situations from which refugees have had to flee, and to adjust the false and distorted image some people in our societies have of them. So this project is based upon the architectural memories of people who have fled their countries and the places they used to inhabit. The shared descriptions of their special places were reimagined in a simple and minimalistic graphical way and are shown in combination with their own narration. This enables the viewer to rethink, reimagine and recreate the places in their own minds.

The Illegal Project

The Illegal Project.
Image: TAB Collective

Urban space has many possibilities and each citizen uses it in their own way. This is especially interesting when it comes to unusual or illegal usage of urban space. These special users create their own strategies for apprehending the space that surrounds them. Urban space is the workplace for drug dealers or prostitutes, it is the habitat for homeless people. They all use public space and the surrounding structures for their benefit. Places become hiding or sleeping spots, urban structures are used as a quiet retreat or as somewhere to shelter from the weather – or the police. The Illegal Project documents this "misuse" of space, but it also questions the current political and bureaucratic agenda and the consequences for certain groups and places. ■

Scenographies of Power

of Power

From the state of exception to the spaces of exception

By Maite Borjabad

As a critical view on how architecture materialises legal frameworks and political apparatuses, Scenographies of Power seeks to disclose, register and reveal the implications of physical space and architectural articulations to the construction of scenarios that not only stage our contemporary political apparatus but also become witnesses of such power structures.

Scenographies of Power is ongoing research that has already produced diverse projects. One of them is the exhibition, shown here, which proposes a reflection upon spaces that materialise the "state of exception" as well as a critical reading of the typologies that these spaces of exception conform to. This exhibition, which took place between June and September 2017 at La Casa Encendida in Madrid, aspired to claim the spatial articulations that make it possible to institute and enforce the state of exception as a tool of power wielded by contemporary political structures. The exhibition – which looks at diplomatic spaces, airports, contested borders and court process – reveals how, within these spatial materialisations of the exception, the aesthetic becomes political.

These spaces of exception are interrogated by different artists, who work with that which takes place within them. They use disruptive propositions to critically represent, record or reactivate, allowing alternative readings of the political framework that hosts each space. The featured works include: *Delivery for Mr. Assange, A Live Mail Art Piece, RRRRRRRRRRRRRRRRADICAL REALTIME!* by !Mediengruppe Bitnik (CH/UK) who sent a package to Julian Assange at his office in the Ecuadorian Embassy in London. It was fitted with a GPS-mode telephone and a camera programmed to take a photo every ten seconds and upload it onto a Twitter account showing a live feed of its journey.

Maite Borjabad

Maite Borjabad is a Spanish architect, researcher and curator working in Chicago and New York. She is currently assistant curator of architecture and design at the Art Institute of Chicago. Previously, she worked at The Metropolitan Museum, and Arthur Ross Architecture Gallery and developed projects at the Emily Harvey Foundation, New Museum Incubator (NY) and La Casa Encendida (Madrid) among others. Her work revolves between architecture, art, politics and diverse forms of critical spatial practices.

Opposite: Scenographies of Power exhibition view. Image: Maria Eugenia Serrano

Another work created by Trevor Paglen (USA) is a sculpture called *Autonomy Cube*, which is a Wi-Fi hotspot that anyone can use wherever it is installed, but unlike normal internet connections it is a Tor relay that routes all of the Wi-Fi traffic over the Tor network, a global network of thousands of volunteer-run relays designed to help anonymise data. When *Autonomy Cube* is installed, both the sculpture, host institution and users become part of a privacy-oriented, volunteer run internet infrastructure.

Contraband, a piece by Taryn Simon (USA), comprises 1,075 photographs taken at both the US Customs and Border Protection Federal Inspection Site and the US Postal Service International Mail Facility at John F. Kennedy International Airport, New York. For one working week, the artist continuously photographed items detained or seized from passengers and express mail entering the United States from abroad.

Something About Contemporary Nomadism is a video installation by Gulnara Kasmalieva and Muratbek Djumaliev (KGZ) that also addresses policing and security measures in border environments in a different context. Their film was shot illicitly in several airports in their home country. The shots from their hidden camera captured not only the quotidian airport ritual of the body search, but also revealed the conditions under which the film was made. Coming from a country with a strong historical tradition of nomadism, the artists comment ironically on its contemporary version.

Scenographies of Power is an invitation to rethink spaces of exception in order to decipher and mobilise the relationship between law and power. The exhibition evinces the affective impact these spaces can have,

alongside their respective legal and political protocols.
Each work in the exhibition approaches the debate from a
specific type of space of exception, reactivating that space
through a subversive action that facilitates alternative
interpretations of the political apparatus in which it is
situated. Thus, *Scenographies of Power* aims to question
these spaces as materialisations-in-progress of the state of
exception, as living spaces that are under construction
and, therefore, can be interrupted, modified, re-articulated
and re-programmed as we challenge the validity of their
political underpinnings. ■

Scenographies of Power
exhibition. Image: Maria
Eugenia Serrano

Radical Hope

Reactionary politics relies on a pessimistic view of the future. It is an inflexible stance that does not encourage new solutions. To hope for a better future is thus a radical act. Real change can only come with hope.

Children
Know

Future architecture
from future architects

By Architectural Thinking
School for Children

The Architectural Thinking School for Children is located in Minsk, Belarus. It teaches architectural thinking as a tool for understanding the contemporary world. Founded in 2016 by architect Alexander Novikov and art historian and designer Elena Karpilova, the idea behind the institution is that extra-curricular education can play a decisive role in a child's future development.

There are 16 studios at the school focusing on a variety of different disciplines – from contemporary art to storytelling to biology – all through an architectural lens. Each studio is tutored by practicing professionals. Today there are around 50 tutors and 80 students, age 7-13, at the school. The main programme takes place over two years. The first year is dedicated to systems thinking and each semester dedicated to one large project, such as the production of a film or book. Students complete each project by progressing through a range of different studios. The second year is dedicated to research. Students take Minsk as their subject, considering it from the perspectives of different disciplines and making their own speculations regarding the future of the city. The result is an interactive map available online at minskeye.by.

The following extracts are project descriptions by second year students asked to design the Apartment House of the Future (2067):

Valery Volodko, aged 11
My building is very compact because of the probable overpopulation in the future. It looks like a frame with cylindrical suspended modules. The building is also envisaged for the end of the world. It is distinguished from the other contemporary buildings by its compactness. The building is made of plastic; power lines are connected to it.

Architectural Thinking School for Children

The Architectural Thinking School for Children was founded in July 2016 by curator and artist Elena Karpilova and architect Alexander Nokikov. Elena Karpilova is a designer, curator, art historian and head of Minsk Design Week. She studied at the Belarusian State University of Culture and Arts as well as the Minsk State Art College. Alexander Novikov is an architect and partner at KARAKO Architecture Studio. He studied at the Strelka Institute for Media, Architecture and Design and the Belarusian National Technical University.

Rescue Module

Opposite: Minsk research

It will be erected on the water (there will be a pole from the bottom). All and everyone will live in it. It is also very easy to buy an apartment in this building. All the modules are very compact. They have everything you need. In case of a hurricane or an earthquake, modules will move down under the water. And if there is no water, the modules will be very tightly pressed against the frame. This means that people are safe. There are ten modules in the building. Each accommodates up to five people.

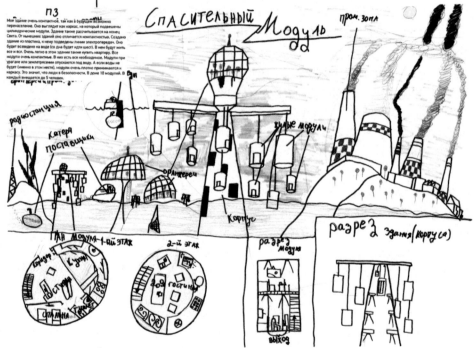

Rescue Module drawing
by Valery Volodko

City of Parks

Zhenya Muravsky, aged 7
My house is glassy, comfortable, strong, big. There is a lot of nature in it and it can fly with the help of wing-engines. Actually, it is a smart palace. Strong and cool people will live in it. My house is made of glass, crystals. There is a horror park on the fifth floor, you can come there and

ПАРКОГНК

ПЛАН ЕЕТОЖА

ГОРОД
ПАРКОВ

City of Parks drawing
by Zhenya Muravsky

laugh if you are feeling moody. I will build this house in
the park. And people with the same name will live there.
It will have 1-20 apartments and there will always be a
lot of sweets in them. The house is too strong. It will not
remind you of anything you've seen before.

Kirill Klebanov, aged 11

Green House – Green Town

I see my project as a big green house. In the future, I
want people to have a lot of space and light. I believe that
people should spend time on the streets and in parks. My
building is "cylinder-expanded"; round, because there are
too many square buildings in big cities. The Green House
is not a prefab panel building. It is deconstructed. And this
building fits Minsk and other green cities perfectly. The
world needs environmental friendliness and my building
meets all standards. The Green Town is provided with
green energy: ultra-solar batteries generate ten times
more electricity than usual. There are also 16 buildings on
one floor, that is 64 apartments and 28,608 people.

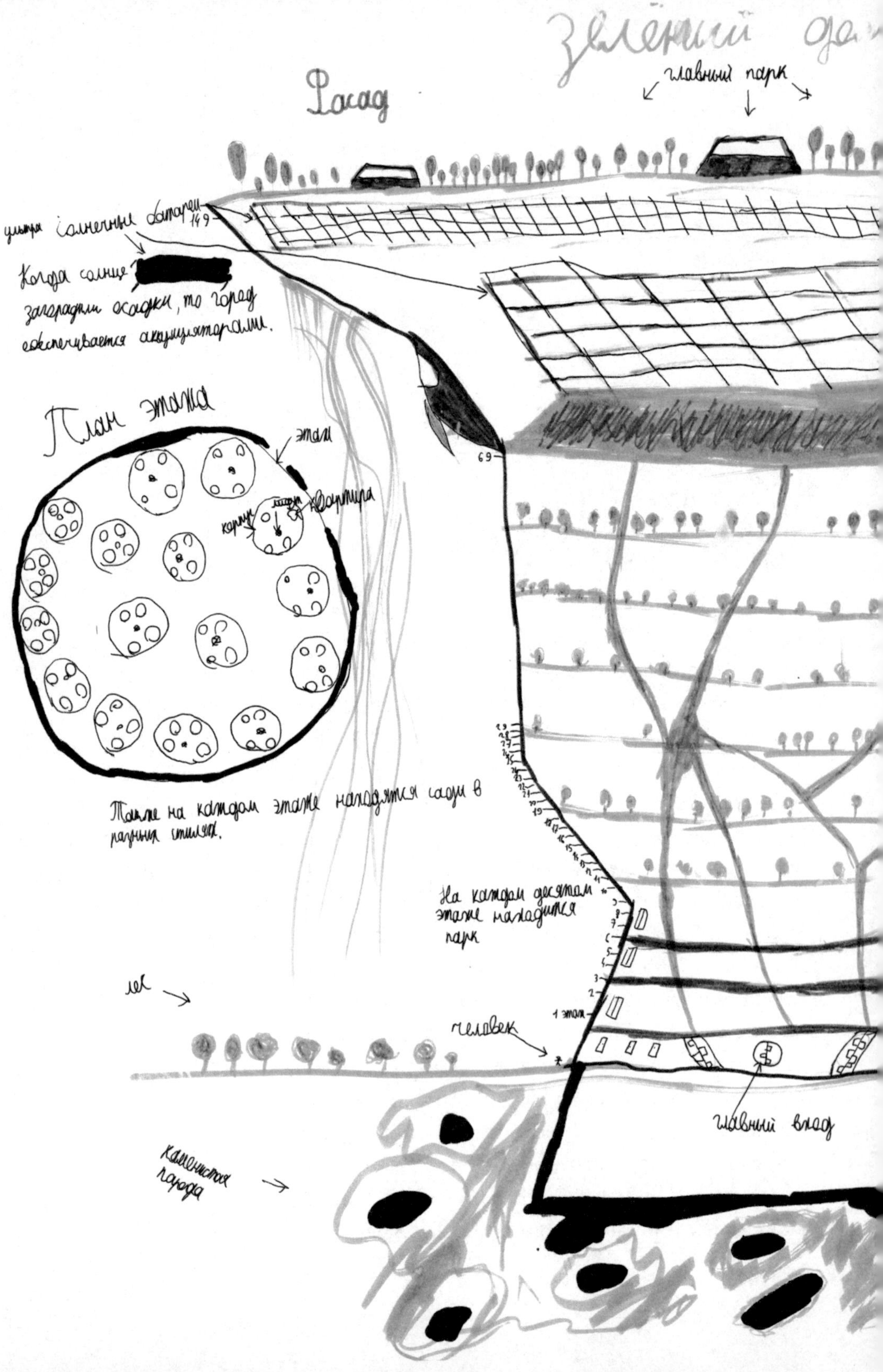

Фасад

Зелёный де...

главный парк

цифра ?солнечные батареи 149

Когда солнце заградили осадки, то город обеспечивается аккумуляторами.

План этажа

этаж

корни ?этаж квартира

Также на каждом этаже находятся сады в разных стилях.

лес →

На каждом десятом этаже находится парк

человек →

3

2

1 этаж

главный вход

каменистая порода →

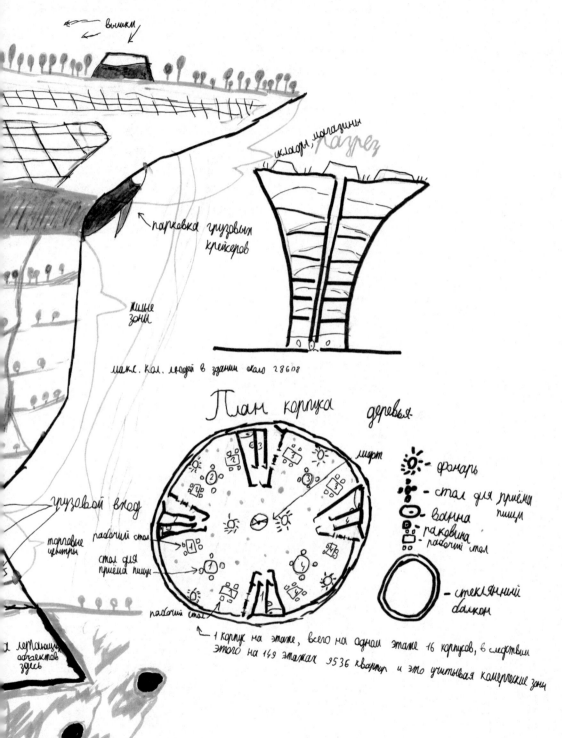

зелёный городок

вышки

Разрез

склады, магазины

парковка грузовых крейсеров

жилые зоны

макс. кол. людей в здании около 28608

План корпуса   деревья

старт

фонарь

- стол для приёма пищи
- ванна
- раковина
- рабочий стол

- стеклянный балкон

грузовой въезд

торговые центры

рабочий стол

стол для приёма пищи

рабочий стол

я леталаздесь объектов здесь

1 корпус на этаже, всего на одном этаже 16 корпусов, в следствии этого на 149 этажах 9536 квартир и это учитывая коммерческие зоны

Above Nature

Anna Bezenson, aged 8

This is a normal standard house. It does not differ from ordinary panel houses. It has a rectangular shape. There will be even more nature by 2067, but my house will not harm it. It is above it. It will produce energy from the sun and lakes. It will be above the forest. Adults and children will live in it. In the adult house there will be a kitchen, a hall, a bedroom, a toilet. In the house of a teenager there will be a hall, a bedroom, a toilet, but without a kitchen, because children do not know how to use kitchen appliances. This is my house.

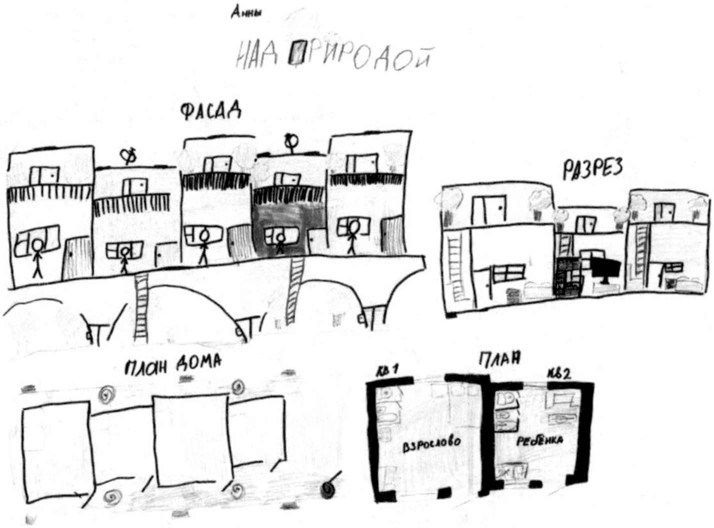

Previous spread:
Green House – Green Town
drawing by Kirill Klebanov

This page: Above Nature
drawing by Anna Bezenson

Snail

Sonia Prudnikova, aged 10

Welcome to the "Snail" ECO-HOUSE! Not many changes will take place in 50 years in Minsk, but the city will become bigger and many forests around the city will be cut down to build houses. That's why I designed Snail ECO-HOUSE, which will not spoil the ecology, but on the contrary – it will restore it.

Who will live in the Snail? People who care about the environment. And, of course, their animals :) They move around the city on electric bicycles or ordinary bicycles. They collect energy during the day and then park in a special parking lot on the 0 floor and give energy to the house.

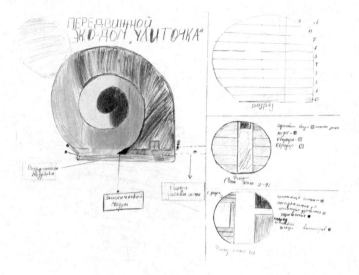

Snail drawing
by Sonia Prudnikova

What kind of house is this? Snail is a technological ten-storey house, which moves on a special air cushion. It is made of organic materials. There are solar panels for heating and electricity installed. The house moves itself to places where nature needs to be to restored. Snail plows the ground and sows the seeds of plants and trees. To do this, there is a floor where the soil, seeds, fertilizers are stored and a special system for sowing is in place. The sewer system is made in such a way that everything is processed into a fertilizer and mixed with soil for seeds, so the plants from Snail grow fast! ■

The Architect as Mediator

Two ways of designing dialogues with European residential communities

A conversation between
the Unfolding Pavilion
and Space Transcribers

The Architect as Mediator

Two ways of designing dialogues with European housing communities

A conversation between the Unfolding Pavilion and Space Transcribers

"Our project is mostly about representation, about making different narratives visible, adding layers of richness to a space, and showing the potential of what is usually seen as a problem."

One of the critics' favourites at the 2018 Venice Architecture Biennale was not even part of the official event. The Unfolding Pavilion on the island of Giudecca transformed an empty apartment in a 1980s social housing block designed by the architect Gino Valle into a reflexive exhibition that aimed to include local residents rather than impose itself upon them. In this conversation, Davide Tommaso Ferrando, Sara Favargiotti and Daniel Tudor Munteanu, three of the curators behind the Unfolding Pavilion, discuss their project with Daniel Pereira and Fernando Ferreira from a network of architects called Space Transcribers, as well the latter's project Transcribe, submitted to the Future Architecture platform Open Call 2017, and which explores the socio-spatial dynamics of another community in Braga, Portugal.

Unfolding Pavilion

The Unfolding Pavilion was curated by Daniel Tudor Munteanu, Davide Tomasso Ferrando, Magda Vierio, Octavian Hrebenciuc and Sara Favargiotti. Daniel Tudor Munteanu is an architect, curator and editor based in Suceava, Romania. Davide Tommaso Ferrando is a researcher, critic and curator based in Innsbruck, Austria. Magda Vieiru and Octavian Hrebenciuc are architects based in Brașov, Romania. Sara Favargiotti is an architect and researcher based in Trento, Italy.

Davide Tommaso Ferrando Daniel and Fernando, can you tell us what Transcribe is about?

Daniel Pereira Transcribe is a one-year project commissioned by the Braga City Council in 2016 and sponsored by EU funding. The project was meant to tackle issues related to three social housing neighbourhoods in Braga that are mostly inhabited by Roma communities, two of which were undergoing a regeneration process: one more infrastructural, one more superficial. The city council asked us to work on the material and the social fabric of these neighbourhoods to bring new narratives to their realities. You can imagine the huge misconceptions that exist around these social housing complexes. People have lived there since the end of the 1970s and not much has changed, so these places are still

Previous Spread:
Giudecca Social Housing.
Image: Laurian Ghinitoiu

related to imaginaries of fear. Our idea was to enter these neighbourhoods, engage with the people and transcribe their reality by means of different kinds of media to allow their complexity to emerge and the city of Braga to acknowledge it. We designed a project divided into phases, the first of which was based on five workshops to be held together with the local communities.

Fernando Ferreira The first phase was about understanding these social housing neighbourhoods, collecting data. Two of them date from the late seventies, the third one is from the late eighties, and none of them was designed by a "star architect". We researched the history of these three neighbourhoods and the migratory movements of their Roma communities.

DP For the second phase, we designed five workshops. Each one was tuned to the specific skills of the members of our NGO: photography, video, audio, model-making and gender mapping. We organised each of the workshops directly with their inhabitants. These people are used to receiving visits from academics who come with inquiries like, "what is your level of satisfaction with the neighbourhood, from 1 to 10?" The inhabitants don't care about these surveys and don't understand why they do them. So, we tried to engage with them in a more emotional and informal way.

FF We were interested in designing dialogues that would help us understand the constraints and the possibilities of these communities. With this information gathered, we could then start to mediate the lack of dialogue that existed between the residents and the public authorities: Bragahabit, the municipal company that holds these three social housing complexes, and Braga City Council.

We tried to maintain an independent position in order to better engage with them.

DP The first time we went to the estates, we went as representatives of the city council and Bragahabit, so the inhabitants started shouting at us, complaining about all the promises made by public institutions that had been broken. So, we understood that we should act as independent mediators.

The workshops followed the idea of taking decision-making powers to the neighbourhoods' stakeholders, since the people from the municipality who are in charge of them don't visit these complexes. Then, in July 2017, we launched an open call for a one-week experimental summer lab to be held in all three estates. The participants had to work with the inhabitants, understand their realities, and propose something performative. Interestingly, each summer lab engaged in a different way with the specific issues of the neighbourhood it addressed. The following phase was the exhibition that we organised inside an abandoned ceramic and glass factory. Here we presented all the material we had produced up to that point. We also exhibited archive photographs of the neighbourhoods from the 1970s that were made public for the first time. They document the precarious conditions in which the Roma communities used to live.

FF They also document, although indirectly, the speculation processes that have transformed the city of Braga during the last decades, showing how places that were once fields and informal settlements are now shopping centres.

Space Transcribers

Daniel Duarte Pereira and Fernando P. Ferreira are architects and co-founders of Space Transcribers. Space Transcribers is a non-profit organization and an international network of architects, urbanites and artists based in Braga, Portugal. Its methodology explores site-specific actions (workshops, events and exhibitions) that engage closely with places' specificities and social dynamics, in a constant quest of contents and processes that can be transcribed into structured narratives.

"The first time we went to the estates the inhabitants started shouting at us."

DTF Did the communities you worked with show up at the exhibition?

DP Some... actually, it was quite hard to bring them to the exhibition. They were all invited, we picked some up, but few came. The most important part of this project was the process, working with the inhabitants. The exhibition was mostly for the people of Braga, many of whom told us they had no idea these realities existed. Also, at the end of the exhibition, we organised a forum, inviting different stakeholders to discuss issues around social housing. And now the final phase is the book, the document that will preserve the legacy of what we did.

DTF Switching to the Unfolding Pavilion: in 2016 Magda, Oti, Daniel and I visited the Giudecca Social Housing complex and immediately fell in love with it, to the extent that we decided to organise an exhibition there for the next Venice Biennale.

In November 2017, after a very long and difficult period of email exchanges with the administration, Sara and I travelled for one week to Venice and managed to visit the apartment that would eventually host the exhibition. As a matter of fact, it was very difficult for us to collaborate with the city council, because we were proposing something completely new to them, and therefore no one wanted to take responsibility for it. Finally, we reached the following agreement: that they would let us organise an exhibition in exchange for us refurbishing – at our own expense – the apartment that hosted it, so that it could be rented out again at the end of the exhibition. Of course, we had mixed feelings about this: on one side, we wondered how they could ask us to take responsibility for a service that they were supposed to provide, but on

"It was difficult for us to collaborate with the city council because no one wanted to take responsibility for it."

the other hand, we understood that we had a very good story to tell, and were excited at the idea of enriching our project with such a strong political meaning.

In March 2018, we finally signed a contract for "free and temporary use" of the apartment. The document didn't allow any residential use, of course, but by sneaking a clause that said the apartment would become an "experimental space for artistic performances", it allowed us to sleep in it during the following months. In the beginning, it really felt like squatting, given the bad conditions in which the apartment had been left. No hot water and no properly working toilets. In the following weeks, nevertheless, we managed to make the apartment look decent enough to host an exhibition. What we couldn't fix ourselves – gas, electricity, and water – was contracted to a private firm, who we could pay thanks to financial support from Innsbruck University.

Bathroom at the Giudecca Social Housing. exhibition. Image: atelier XYZ

Sara Favargiotti We painted the walls and louvres, we cleaned the apartment and the outside spaces, and did some gardening. In the beginning, the neighbours weren't particularly happy, mainly because of the noise we were producing. But after a few days, many understood and appreciated what we were doing, to the point that in the end we became friends with some of them. We had interesting conversations in the common spaces of the complex. They shared with us how their sense of community had changed, remembering parties and barbecues all together. From my point of view, our project has somehow re-activated this lost sense of community by giving all of them something to be interested in: something to care for and discuss.

DTF During these few months we connected with about twenty inhabitants. We kept them informed about what we were doing with leaflets left in their mailboxes. However, during the days of the exhibition only a few of them joined us. Those who came visited the apartment and some of them followed the events, but we expected more participation. One thing that has to be stressed, still, is that the most important ingredient of our project was the extraordinary quality of the building.

Daniel Tudor Munteanu The Giudecca social housing complex is by a well-known Italian architect, Gino Valle, who used to be a professor in Venice, so both he and his building are well known in the city. It's a sort of mat-building made of pavilions clustered around private patios and public squares. What struck me, when I first visited it, was that nobody used those public spaces. Probably the reason is that most of the inhabitants are still the original ones. They are now elderly and spend more time inside their homes. Interestingly, the installations that we exhibited occupied both the apartment and public

spaces, and the latter were the most welcomed by the
inhabitants. Many were pretty sad when they learned we
were going to remove them. Indeed, we always wanted
to work on an exhibition that was going to be attractive
not only for architects but also for the inhabitants of the
complex. In this sense, I believe it worked, even if during
the three days of events, which had a very casual and
informal mood, they preferred to stay towards the margins.

Kids playing in the public
garden at Picoto, Braga.
Image: Fernando Ferreira

DP Regarding the liveliness of these neighbourhoods: we
all studied architecture and we always have in mind images
of Nigel Anderson, Team X, Robin Hood Gardens and social
housing complexes full of kids playing... When we think of
collectiveness we think of people using these spaces. But the
truth is that nowadays it is very hard to find lively places that
don't involve shopping centres. You need to have something
that makes people want to go there. Nevertheless, when we
first went to the Picoto estate, for example, the situation was
different, almost picturesque. We saw a lot of kids playing
and could actually feel the collectiveness. This is probably
related to the fact that Roma communities are really close.
They gather together and use public spaces a lot.

Previous spread: Photography
workshop at Picoto, Braga.
Image: Daniel Pereira

FF But I believe it is also related to the morphology of the building and to the scale of the public spaces. Our reality in Braga is very different from the one in Giudecca. Valle's project is really great and, in some sense, reminds me of the Barbican, but it is very different from our reality, because the scale of our social housing neighbourhoods is much more human.

DP I must say I am quite sceptical about this. Most modern architects were optimistic about the idea of community and collectiveness. But this is a failure that we have inherited from that era. We can design collectiveness, beautiful typologies and patios, but people don't go there if you don't put a Starbucks inside. I think architects, in this sense, live closed in the idea that if you design quality spaces, people will follow. I feel that this is not true. What I find interesting, instead, is the question of strategy: not thinking only in terms of space, but also in terms of programme. Maybe a patio could be a place to organise dinners, in a certain moment, and in another, it could be turned into an urban garden. Architects might not even design space, but programmes for spaces.

"We have to open space to indeterminacy: spaces must be flexible to allow their appropriation."

FF We have to open space to indeterminacy: spaces must be flexible to allow their appropriation. In Braga it was very interesting to observe how the communities appropriate the balconies, for example, and the other public spaces. Hanging clothes there and so on. In modernist buildings appropriation and the possibility to play with public space has been lost.

DP I don't think it has been lost, I think they have transitioned. Collectiveness, today, seems like a premise – something that everybody agrees on and nobody questions. But do we want collectiveness? Do we want everybody to be together and do stuff together? Do we want a dialogue to exist? We think this is right. We think we have to create a dialogue between the administration and the inhabitants, that they have to agree. But is that the way?

FF I see two realities here: that of Venice, which I correlate with the Barbican, and that of Braga. And to me they are two different realities. What I have seen in the Barbican, where I studied the issue of solitude, is that people were always alone in the public spaces. What maybe needs to be capitalised upon is programming public space as you tried to do with your exhibition in Venice. You programme the events and provide an opportunity for the residents to take part in them, if they want. You need a catalyst, and then you see what happens – whether the people join or not.

"Do we want collectiveness? Do we want everybody to be together and do stuff together?"

An installation from the Unfolding Pavilion in the Giudecca Social Housing. Image: atelier XYZ

DTF In our case, programming "activities" in the collective spaces of the Giudecca social housing was very important, because nothing had happened in those spaces for years, and the inhabitants told us they were fascinated to see hundreds of people walking around their everyday places. This made them see their own home with different eyes. The same effect was produced by placing site-specific installations in those spaces and also by re-telling the story of the building by means of an exhibition dedicated to it. In a more or less planned way we managed to temporarily change the programme, the imaginary and the space of the Giudecca social housing. At the beginning of the project, the vast majority of the conversations we

Giudecca Social Housing.
Image: ZA² (Emiliano Zandri
and Lorenzo Zandri)

had with the inhabitants would be about how badly the building was built, how many problems they had with the vertical typology of its apartments, the narrowness and steepness of the staircases, and so on. Problems that still exist, of course. But the very same people, during the days of the exhibition, would tell us how privileged they were to live in such a special and beautiful place. The fact is, the way you see a place also depends on the things that are said about it.

DP Yes, that's the power of representation, of making something visible. Actually, I think our project is mostly about representation, about making different narratives visible, adding layers of richness to a space, and showing the potential of what is usually seen as a problem. We don't design in the traditional sense, but what I see is that architects work really well as mediators: we know how to deal with different people with different skills.

FF Yes, because we have a perspective that makes us different from sociologists, anthropologists and social workers: the skill of representing, of making visible things to different kinds of public. For us, this was the goal of the whole project.

DP And in this sense, our two projects are related. It is not so much about the final outcome, but about the process. Of course, we are all happy about what we did, but the story of how we managed to do it, how things can be done in a different way, is more important.

FF Regarding the legacy of these projects, we are totally aware that we are just touching the tip of a huge iceberg. First, as you can imagine, the social housing neighbourhoods we worked with have many complex

dynamics and problems related to many fields such as
politics, economics, architecture, sociology, and so on.
We are aware that, during this phase, we can at least
try to make these problems visible to the city and other
entities. Now the idea is to continue and make this seed
grow, in order to produce changes in the way in which
these neighbourhoods are perceived, and in the way in
which urban regeneration is usually approached.

DP I could say that the legacy doesn't come from us. Some
residents of the Santa Tecla complex, for example, recently
took part in an event in Braga proposing the creation of
an office between them and the city council to mediate
during the ongoing regeneration. When I spoke with some
of the people who participated they told me that the project
we did together helped them see that they needed this kind
of mediation. I believe that this is a legacy of our project.

DTF To be honest, despite the fact that we refurbished
one apartment and that this will be given back to the city,
we know this doesn't change the situation in Venice. We
discovered that there are hundreds of public apartments
that are empty, just like ours, which is clearly a problem.
What I can say at least, is that thanks to the Biennale and
the media coverage our story received we had the chance
to communicate to a wider international audience that this
situation exists.

DTM You cannot solve the problems of a city through a
building or an exhibition, that's clear. But you can draw
the focus of the media and others on to a specific problem,
hoping that your action will ignite a solution.

DTF Regarding budget, how much money did your project
cost?

DP The entire package, from research to the book, came to a little under 70,000 EUR.

DTF This is a very big difference between our two projects. Whilst yours has been a one-year, full time commitment, we didn't earn any money from it. We reinvested all the funds we gathered into the project itself. But how to make this a job is also an important question.

FF The possibility to change this has to do with the political system. In our experience, we obtained the the funding to do this project after an initial, pro-bono experience. We were very proactive, we did a workshop in which we organised everything, and the municipality realised it was something interesting. After two years they invited us to repeat the experience, but this time with public funds. It is very important to be in touch with the political system, with people who manage the city. In this case, we were quite lucky because we met a coordinator who supported us a great deal.

DP It is about people. You need the city council, but you also need this one person who invites you and believes in you, someone who will help you in the end. From the beginning, we made clear that we would only work on the project if it was funded. At the same time, we anticipated that some of the results of our project could have cast a bad light on the municipality of Braga, regarding the way in which it deals with social housing, and they accepted that. We were quite lucky.

FF That happens in all kinds of projects. If you can connect to the people you work with, the work flows. In this case, the coordinator trusted us even though she didn't know us. She just liked what we did.

"It is very important to be in touch with the political system, with people who manage the city."

SF In our case, we invited the people from the City Council of Venice, those who gave us the key to the apartment, to join our activities, and of course to take part in the opening event. Unfortunately, no one came. We don't understand why and it is, of course, a pity.

DTF Now I realise that our two projects are very different. You directly tackled the issues of the communities you worked with. You had a clear intention to work on the social dimension. For us, this was more of an outcome, since we first and foremost worked as curators who have to prepare a venue for an exhibition. It is interesting to see how both projects end up being architectural, but from very different points of view.

Model making workshop, Picoto, Braga. Image: Fernando Ferreira

DTM One more thing that I would like to add, is that our activity is to be read in the context of the Architecture Biennale, and that we really tried to do things in an unusual way. If you are part of the Biennale you organise exhibitions, which take a huge amount of time and require huge budgets, and you are always constrained by the Biennale logo and the institutions that sponsor your activities. We, on the other hand, were doing things independently.

DP Were you not part of the programme of the Biennale?

DTM No, but we made it in time for the vernissage. By being there in that precise moment, people perceived us as being part of the Biennale. But the point is that if you want to have the Biennale logo in order to be an official collateral event, you need to pay a 15,000 EUR fee. Instead, with half of that budget, we managed to organise our exhibition. I think that in a way we are showing that things can be done differently by focusing only on what is important.

DP That is a statement. I didn't know that, and I find it very subversive.

DTF In this sense, I find it quite funny to see so many people going to the Venice Biennale, taking part in its vernissages, dinners and parties, and then complaining about how superficial and useless this all is. I am happy that the Biennale exists! Without it, we would have never been able to organise the Unfolding Pavilion, as it is the importance of the Biennale that allows you to gather funds and people in one place. So if one specific edition of the Biennale is bad (like this year's, I would say), we should of course criticise it. But I wouldn't blame the Biennale. The Biennale as a tool is a very good tool: it all depends on how you use it. ■

"If you want to have the Biennale logo in order to be an official collateral event, you need to pay a 15,000 EUR fee."

Symbiocene

Working with weeds

By Trajna Collective

Symbiocene is a nomadic platform set up by our interdisciplinary collective, Trajna. Symbiocene questions our design sensibilities and produces work and experiments that function outside the anthropocentric production of everyday realities. Continuously evolving, it aims to explore the potentials of interspecies collaboration and look for ways to encourage symbiotic relationships. We believe that the ongoing extinction of different life forms obliges us to resuscitate synergic relationships between living beings. The project's main goal is thus to design resilient cityscapes by exploring the dynamics of interspecies existence within urban landscapes.

Many polluted and degraded ecosystems have become thriving homes for invasive plants. As a consequence of global trade and traffic, these displaced species alter newly conquered ecosystems and threaten our biodiversity. They forcefully remind us of the necessity to question our anthropocentric perspectives on economies, habitation and land. Symbiocene utilises the material and symbolic qualities of these species to initiate land restoration, ethical economies and spaces for multispecies learning, thereby showcasing ways to transform competitive relations into symbiotic ones.

One of our most promising projects is NotWeed, a paper product made from invasive plants. According to the Food and Agriculture organisation of the United Nations (FAO), global tree plantations have expanded by more than 50 percent in the past 30 years. In order to protect planetary biodiversity, we need to find sustainable alternatives to standardised processes of paper pulp production. Together with volunteers in Ljubljana we have been foraging thriving weeds from urban wastelands and using them as an alternative source of cellulose in half-industrial paper

Trajna Collective

Symbiocene was set up by design duo Gaja Mežnarić Osole and Andrej Koruza who work within the Trajna collective.

Gaja Mežnarić Osole is a Ljubljana-based designer. After finishing a master's degree in systemic design at Goldsmiths in London, she started working in cross-disciplinary fields between design, ecology and participation.

Andrej Koruza attended the Mosaic School of Friuli. His interdisciplinary practice consists of leading the production and wood workshop in a collective of designers, architects and craftsmen, producing various mosaic installations and creating installations.

Opposite: Trajna Collective foraging Japanese knotwood. Image: Trajna Collective

Above: Trajna Collective
foraging Japanese knotwood.
Image: Nataša Košmerl

Bellow: The production
of NotWeed paper.
Image: Trajna Collective

production. Our locally produced, chlorine-free paper gives us and our paper users an opportunity to join the efforts of preserving natural resources and to become part of an inventive solution to the issue of invasive plants.

Another project concerning the creation of community spaces for learning, experimentation and making is called Embodied Knowledge Shelters. We recognise the importance of collective action when tackling the problems of the anthropocene and so decided to activate public spaces and mobilise cultural institutions to facilitate education about local ecosystems and their resilience in relation to global environmental change. We host workshops, lectures and other community gatherings, learning how and with whom to cooperate and build a diverse web of life in our future cities. At one of these events we used scrap wood from a Tree of Heaven (*Ailanthus altissima)* to transform an exhibition space into a temporary working studio, which became a venue for our design work, weekly meetings, lectures, workshops and presentations on beekeeping practices. The studio was fitted with furniture elements we made from the biomass of invasive plants. At the end of the exhibition, the furniture pieces were auctioned off, funding the development and continuation of the project.

A third project, Groundworks, involved landscape restoration. In one of Ljubljana's city parks we are actively removing invasive Tree of Heaven biomass, organising reading sessions there, and investigating uses for the collected biomass. Currently we are looking for ways to use it as a substrate for growing edible mushrooms. By employing permaculture principles, scientific research, participatory methods and creative skills, we are looking at transforming damaged ecosystems into playgrounds of diverse human and extra-human economies. ■

What is a
School if not
a Promise?

**Radical hope
at the Floating University**

By George Kafka

What is a school if not a promise?
Radical hope at the Floating University

By George Kafka

"We know that there are lots of people around in academia that are looking for other ways of dealing with the real world."

"What is a school if not a promise?" asked Ethel Baraona Pohl and César Reyes of dpr-barcelona, and Rosario Talevi of the Open Raumlabor University, on the occasion of the 2018 Istanbul Design Biennial, entitled "School of Schools". There they staged a collaborative Parasitic Reading Room that aimed to provoke "a contagion of knowledge" as it roamed the city. The school, as a nebulous site and idea, is at the centre of much of dpr-barcelona and raumlaborberlin's work – as is a profound optimism. This manifests itself not in a blindness or naivety, but in a grounded practicality: trust in the abilities of others and the inkling that a radical future is just around the corner. Another project, the Floating University, was initiated by raumlabor in Berlin and was imbued with the same spirit. Here, the promise of a school collided with Berlin's urban politics and water infrastructure on a floating structure inflated with radical hope.

On the north side of Tempelhofer Feld, an airport-turned-park in southern Berlin, lies a large ditch. Surrounded by lots and bungalows and noticeable only to those in the know, this nineteenth-century basin holds rainwater drained from the airport's defunct runways before it is fed into Berlin's canal network.

"We knew it was kind of a secret spot in the centre of the city that nobody had on the map," explains Benjamin Foerster-Baldenius of raumlaborberlin architects. That is, until this summer.

From April to September 2018, the basin was occupied by a peculiar, offshore structure – a constellation of scaffolded

George Kafka

George Kafka is a writer, editor and researcher based in London. He is a founding member of &beyond and deputy editor at *Thinking City*. He has written about architecture and cities for *The Architectural Review, Disegno, Blueprint, Metropolis* and *Frieze*, among others.

Previous spread: water laboratory at the Floating University. Image: Victoria Tomaschko, courtesy of raumlaborberlin

volumes and floating platforms with inflatable rooftops and a large wheel. It was part pirate ship and part Princeton; part Archigram and part Burning Man. This was the Floating University, the brainchild of Foerster-Baldenius, Florian Stirnemann and raumlaborberlin, and the locus of a number of events throughout the summer – architectural, educational, and otherwise – that hopped aboard the floating structure.

The Floating University. Image: Lena Giovanazzi, courtesy of Making Futures Bauhaus+

Funded by the German Federal Cultural Foundation as part of its ongoing Bauhaus centenary celebrations, the university was initiated by raumlaborberlin as a continuation and expansion on its previous education experiments such as the Osthang Summer School (2014), Urban School Ruhr (2016-17), and Making Futures Bauhaus+ (2018, in cooperation with the University of the Arts, Berlin). In these cases, raumlaborberlin has taken its signature playful and process-focused approach to architecture and urban planning to broaden the often rigid or exclusionary nature of education.

"We know that there are lots of people around in academia that are looking for other ways of dealing with the real world," explains Foerster-Baldenius. "Ways of getting together and finding things out together, not only within the campus, but also more open to the public."

This public-facing approach gave the Floating University its architectural form and a truly unique series of spaces. From a dusty side road, a small gate led visitors onto a metal staircase with a balcony overlooking the basin, giving a dramatic first glimpse of the university structure. Through a thicket of tomato and potato planters, a waterside walkway led to the centre of the structure. Here, a 100-seat auditorium (with a separate floating floor) stood beneath an inflated tarpaulin roof.

The auditorium.
Image: Lena Giovanazzi, courtesy of Making Futures Bauhaus+

Elsewhere, a modular kitchen was designed by architecture students and other participants of a workshop on the socio-spatial history of the kitchen. An innovative water filtration system, designed by artist-in-residence Katherine

" It was part pirate ship
and part Princeton;
part Archigram
and part Burning Man."

Bell, used a wheel to draw the ditch water through a series of interconnected bathtubs containing biological filters such as sand-biofilm, mushroom mycelium and zebra mussels. Located at the back of the auditorium, the manual operation of the wheel took place every hour, creating a constant reminder of the bizarre surroundings. The transparency of the workings of the structure and its semi-natural location were a central part of the experimental education taking place on the site: "It's really hard to stay serious because there's this nature theatre around you, which is just so funny," says Foerster-Baldenius.

Previous Spread: Floating University opening night. Image: Victoria Tomaschko, courtesy of raumlaborberlin

Current page: Water filter system (detail) by Katherine Bell. Image: Lena Giovanazzi, courtesy of Making Futures Bauhaus+

Over the summer, 25 affiliated universities – hailing from Bogotá to Paris – plugged into the structure for experimental seminars and workshops, while a parallel public programme drew Berliners and visitors into discussions spanning urbanism, experimental sound art, water consumption and the legacy of the Bauhaus. On a given Saturday afternoon one might find kids stomping around in the swamp (rubber boots provided) and out-of-towners touring the site whilst attendees joined a performance circling the ditch, enjoyed drinks at the bar, served lunch, got a haircut or listened to a lecture by Forensic Architecture's Eyal Weizman – all at the same time.

Despite the resounding success of the university in expanding design education and opening public infrastructure to new uses, the project's funding ran out at the end of the summer and deconstruction of the university began in September.

This is not, however, the end of the story.

Over the course of its existence the project gained interest and support from city politicians, local media and, thanks to a final Floating Symposium (that ended, of course, on the floating dance floor) to discuss the future of the structure, plans are underway for it to set sail again in 2019.

As Markus Bader, also of raumlaborberlin, explains, "The Floating University is an experiment on many levels. Since the experiment was so successful, many people are now working on a possible next season."

Initial discussions are centred around synchronising the contributions of the different visiting universities, so that each one adds something new to the ever-evolving site. "The Floating University is not the object," says Bader. "It's the spirit and the amazing collectivity that was started this summer."

Foerster-Baldenius is equally optimistic for the future of the basin site itself: "The city is dealing with the surrounding gardens to develop something new out of it and we would like to have a word in this development. We've opened up an area in the city that was asleep for 50 years, and now we have a responsibility for it." * ■

"The Floating University is not the object. It's the spirit and the amazing collectivity that was started this summer."

* An earlier version of this article was published on *Metropolis* (metropolismag.com), 4 October 2018.

Between Consensus and Dissent

An ongoing apocalyptic process requires constant negotiation. If reached, consensus may not last. But dissent and conflict are two different things. There are many benefits to agreeing to disagree.

Commoning
with a small c

On the benefits
of agreeing
to disagree

TORRE
DAVID

By Stefan Gruber
and Anh-Linh Ngo

"Commoning is understood as an arena for encountering and confronting differences."

Commoning with a small c
On the benefits of agreeing to disagree

By Stefan Gruber and Anh-Linh Ngo

Deriving from "the commons", the term used for shared resources both material and immaterial, commoning as a verb describes the processes of sharing and negotiating access to the commons. In this text, two of the curators behind the "An Atlas of Commoning" exhibition and publishing project assert the importance of conflict and dissent within that process. In doing so they bring politics and confrontation back to the forefront of the architecture agenda and present the historic notion of "sharing" without ownership as a basis for intercultural understanding.

Stefan Gruber

Stefan Gruber is the Lucian & Rita Caste Assistant Professor of Architecture and Urbanism at Carnegie Mellon University, where he directs the Master of Urban Design program. His office STUDIOGRUBER works at the intersection of architecture, urbanism and research. He co-authored *Space of Commoning* (Sternberg 2016), *The Report* (MAK 2015) and *Big! Bad? Modern:* (Park 2015) and most recently guest edited and co-curated *An Atlas of Commoning* with ARCH+.

The literary critic H. Bruce Franklin once accused J.G. Ballard (the writer who perhaps best incarnates the apocalyptic imagination of Anglo-American culture) of "mistaking the end of capitalism for the end of the world".[1] He went on to ask: "What could Ballard create if he were able to envision the end of capitalism as not the end, but the beginning, of a human world?"[2] Contemporary apocalyptic thoughts are fuelled by accelerating waves of environmental devastation, aggressive privatisation and political polarisation. But they are just as much the product of a crisis of imagination – our collective inability to project alternative social forms of life beyond contemporary forms of domination.

Against this backdrop, the commons debate has emerged as a positive affirmation of another possible world – a radical imagination that ties many seemingly disparate citizen-led initiatives together in a search for a self-determined existence beyond the influence of the market and state. The verb "commoning" describes the collaborative processes surrounding the (re)production of material

1 Franklin, H. Bruce. "What are we to make of J.G. Ballard's Apocalypse?" in Thomas Claerson (ed.) *Voices for the Future – Essays on major Science Fiction writers,* jgballard.ca/criticism/ballard_apocalypse_1979.html (accessed September 3, 2018)

2 Ibid.

Previous spread: An Atlas of Commoning exhibition view at Kunstraum Kreuzberg/ Bethanien in Berlin, summer 2018. Image: Sebastian Schels

and immaterial common goods. But as is to be expected, in practice, emancipation from prevailing power structures is rarely free of conflict. Commons are subjected to a continuous process of enclosure and re-appropriation in a contested field claimed by a variety of ideologies. Thus, rather than being defined by consensus and suggesting that differences can or should be overcome, commoning is understood as an arena for encountering and confronting differences. Such understanding of the commons is inspired by political theorist Chantal Mouffe's definition of agonism.[3] In her work, Mouffe argues that a pluralist democracy can only exist as long as there is conflict, as long as standing arrangements can be contested.

3 See Mouffe, Chantal. *On the Political.* London: Psychology Press, 2005, pp. 29-34.

"A pluralist democracy can only exist as long as there is conflict."

Mouffe thus challenges the widespread conception of public space as the terrain where consensus can or should emerge. In an agonistic relation, adversaries accept a set of democratic procedures and enter a common symbolic space within which hegemonic conflict takes place. The goal then is to transform antagonism into agonism, while establishing a common respect for irreconcilable differences. Recognising the conflictual nature of coming together and negotiating a common ground, commoning unfolds with an expressed sensitivity towards the exclusionary dimension of an idea of community derived from collective identity. Similarly, commoners should be cautious about nostalgic notions of community rooted in projections of an idealised past, when public space was thriving and social negotiation seemed intact. Instead, commoning as social practice emanates from the negotiation between declared goals and the everyday realities of situated collective practices. The spatial manifestation of such struggle can be traced along three exemplary axes of tension: *Ownership – Access, Production – Reproduction, Right – Solidarity.*

The commons fundamentally challenge prevalent notions of ownership. Today, the instant access to ideas, goods, and services – in contrast to permanent ownership – opens up new possibilities of societal coexistence. Thereby, sharing is no longer necessarily associated with personal sacrifice. What's more, new forms of sharing offer promising approaches that promote a more resource-friendly existence. However, the current transformation of sharing into the sharing economy bears the risk of exacerbating precarious working conditions and social exclusion. Platform capitalism and the hyper-commercialisation of every aspect of life deny a growing, marginalised portion of society access to resources that are essential for life and cultural development. Air, water, and food, but also land (and housing) are such contested resources. For architects and planners, this entails the responsibility of taking a clear position in the struggle over the collective right to the city. Meanwhile *urban commons* should be understood beyond the notion of "liberated enclaves" or alternative islands of resistance, and tackle questions of scale, duration, and structural change.

Anh-Linh Ngo

Anh-Linh Ngo is an architect, author and publisher of ARCH+ magazine. He is co-founder of the international initiative *projekt bauhaus*, which critically examines the ideas of the Bauhaus through symposiums, workshops, pop-up exhibitions and performances from 2015-2019. In 2009 he co-curated the touring exhibition *Post_Oil City*. He co-initiated and co-curated *An Atlas of Commoning.*

Ownership – Access

BITTE SCHUHE
AUSZIEHEN

PLEASE TAKE
OFF SHOES

Previous spread: Information about the 25 projects included in the exhibition installation, the first additions to an ongoing visual "atlas" of commoning. Image: Sebastian Schels

4 See Stavrides, Stavros. *Common Space: the City as Commons.* London: Zed Books, 2016, pp. 4-5.

Stavros Stavrides sees common space as a non-enclosed threshold space, but one that needs threshold institutions to ensure that commoning remains an open process.[4] In common space, in space produced and used as common, people do not simply use an area given by an authority (local state, state, public institution, etc.). People actually mould this kind of space according to their collective needs and aspirations. Whereas public space necessarily has the mark of an identity – it *is*, that's to say it belongs to, the authority – common space tends to be constantly redefined: commons space *happens* and is shaped through collective action. One challenge of the commons discourse is solving the dilemma of institutionalisation. In Stavrides' opinion, only a continual process of negotiation can prevent the accumulation and consolidation of power and counteract mechanisms of exclusion. Accordingly, beyond the mere sharing of material or natural resources, commoning is a continuous and active practice, commoning is a verb.

Production – Reproduction

Beyond challenging the orthodoxy of property, the commons debate contests the separation of functions established by modernism, between living and working or public and private. Instead it seeks new collective forms of living, beyond the paradigms of the twentieth century, which were built upon the foundations of gender politics and domestic labour. Globally, women still perform the majority of unpaid care work and social reproduction. A critical feminist examination of the Marxist economy exposes domestic labour as a hidden form of productive work.[5] The making invisible of unpaid reproductive labour here only serves as one example from an entire arsenal of strategies through which capitalism externalises costs. More commonly, geographic remoteness helps to render the overconsumption of resources, environmental

5 See J. K. Gibson-Graham, *The End of Capitalism (As We Knew It): A Feminist Critique of Political Economy,* University of Minnesota Press, Minneapolis, 2006, pp. 79-101.

devastation and human exploitation invisible as well,
conveniently dissociating our actions from immediate

responsibility. The commons debate counters this approach
with a broader, more diverse definition of economy,
in which all forms of work – paid and unpaid, productive
and reproductive – are recognised as creating value. Kim
Trogal points out that care work itself is a form of spatial
production. Thus, the experiments on the socialisation
of domestic labour in the nineteenth and early twentieth
century entail "new kinds of domestic workspace,
cooperative forms of organisation and architectures".[6]
Similarly, Silvia Federici argues that emancipation must
primarily be directed towards the gender-hierarchical
division of labour and the dependence of market-based
production relations in the kitchen.[7] Only when the
domestic sphere becomes an arena of collective political
life, and collective forms of reproductive labour form
the basis of social reproduction, can alternative forms

One of the exhibitions
thematic islands, this one
exploring "Production
– Reproduction". Image:
Sebastian Schels

6 Torgal, Kim. "Caring:
Making Commons, Making
Connections" in *The Social
(Re)Production of Architecture:
Politics, Values and Actions in
Contemporary Practice*, Doina
Petrescu, Kim Trogal, eds. New
York, Routledge, 2017, p. 163.

7 See Federici, Silvia.
"Feminism and the Politics
of the Common in an Era
of Primitive Accumulation"
(2010), in *Revolution at Point
Zero: Housework, Reproduction,
and Feminist Struggle*, ed.
Silvia Federici. Oakland,
CA: PM Press, 2012, p. 147.

of economic activity – based on solidarity, commons, and sufficiency – become effective in a lasting way. For architecture this means overcoming the dichotomy of public versus private: spatial boundaries need to be renegotiated, domestic activities need to extend into the public sphere, and, conversely, cooperative care should lead to new typologies of community.

Right – Solidarity

The House of One project is the world's first house of prayer for three religions: Christianity, Islam and Judaism. Architects: Kuehn Malvezzi, model: Martin Edelmann (ifa). Image: Sebastian Schels

But how can communities expand their influence and move beyond localised initiatives? Many concepts of the commons are centred on the definition of a specific community that (re)produces, owns, maintains, and shares the commons. This raises the question of belonging to a community of *commoners*. Inevitably, this also places commoning in a problematic tradition: in contrast to the concept of society, the idea of community traditionally designates a group that is unified by a collective identity and constituted by mechanisms of exclusion and demarcation.

The term, however, doesn't only have an exclusionary dimension, it is also anti-modern: Zygmunt Bauman pointed out that it clings to the narrative of a loss of community in which societal change causes a decline in communality.[8] Consequently, the German sociologist Ferdinand Tönnies' early twentieth century writings on the relationship between community and society were compatible with the identitarian trends that culminated in the *Volksgemeinschaft* chimera of Nazism.[9] Today, right wing conservatives and the new right are once again invoking the notion of the community. On the other hand, representatives of the left spectrum bemoan increasing individualisation and fading solidarity in society and are therefore developing alternative concepts of commoning. Juliane Spitta investigates this precarious interpretation of community, which oscillates between appropriation by identitarian and emancipatory movements.[10] In her opinion, a reference to the fiction of the community can only be emancipatory when we overcome the narrow bounds of identitarian affiliation and think in terms of solidarity and globalism. Thus, the politics of commoning should be aimed towards "increasing freedom and agency" for those who don't yet belong. As the pervasive effects of global capitalism continue to spread, the claim for a collective right to the city inevitably implies fighting for a right to the world.

"The claim for a collective right to the city inevitably implies fighting for a right to the world."

8 See Bauman, Zygmunt. *Community: Seeking Safety in an Insecure World.* Cambridge: Polity, Year: 2001, p. 9.

9 See Tonnies, Ferdinand. *Community and Society,* trans. Charles P. Loomis. New York: Harper, 1963), pp. 47, 65.

10 See Spitta, Juliane. The Fiction of Communiy in *An Atlas of Commoning,* eds. Ngo, Anh-Linh, Stefan Gruber et al. Berlin, ARCH+, 2018, p. 20.

11 See Gruber, Stefan. "Designing Commoning Institutions: The Dilemma of the Vienna Settlers, the Commoners, and the Architect" in *Spaces of Commoning*, Baldauf, Anette, Stefan Gruber et al. (eds.), Berlin: Sternberg Press, 2016, p.89.

12 Federici, "Feminism and the Politics of the Common in an Era of Primitive Accumulation," see note 5.

Understood as spaces for agonistic encounter, commoning opens up the possibility of an architecture that is a product as much as it is a process: the cyclical process of negotiating the social (re-)production of space. Architecture renders material our social practices, relations, and values. In turn, the disposition of space defines us. If we can agree on such (albeit non-linear) correlation, architecture can be more than a vehicle for reproducing prevalent power structures, but in fact a potent vehicle for renegotiating social relations. Meanwhile, such negotiation does not begin with architecture. Instead it begins at point zero, with the repetition of everyday practices that over time form patterns and habits, before they consolidate into norms and institutions, and are finally rendered material through architecture.[11] Along those lines, Federici argues that it is only by putting the reproduction of the everyday at the centre of political struggles that the commons movement will gain the capacity to endure: "We cannot build an alternative society and a strong self-reproducing movement unless we redefine our reproduction in a more cooperative way and put an end to the separation between the personal and the political, and between political activism and the reproduction of everyday life."[12] Just as the apocalypse will not occur as a sudden event, so are practices of commoning grounded in the barely visible gestures of day-to-day reality. If we seek to build resilience through commoning, according to Federici, it will always begin with a small c. ■

Stefan Gruber and Anh-Linh Ngo are two of the curators of the exhibition *An Atlas of Commoning*, an ifa-exhibition (Institut für Auslandsbeziehungen) produced in collaboration with the German architecture magazine ARCH+ and research partner Carnegie Mellon University. The exhibition opened in Berlin during the summer of 2018 before going on world tour. Parts of this text have been edited and rearranged from the editorial by Stefan Gruber and Anh-Linh Ngo "The Contested Fields of Commoning" in *An Atlas of Commoning*, eds. Ngo, Anh-Linh, Stefan Gruber et al. Berlin, ARCH+, 2018, pp. 4-5, as well as the essay by Stefan Gruber, "One of Many Atlases to Come..." in the same issue, pp. 44-47.

If These Walls Could Talk

Deconstructing architectures of separation

By RESOLVE

In 2017 the interdisciplinary collective RESOLVE initiated a series of labs with students from East London, called If These Walls Could Talk. Participants were challenged to design a response to the question: what if walls brought us together? Working collaboratively with the team of eight students, the collective realised the response and exhibited it at the Stockwell Festival that year.

Walls, a central element in the discipline of architecture, have long been archetypes of separation. It is through separation that walls traditionally create domestic space; defending the privacy of our homes from the openness of the commons whilst preserving the function of one room from the contents, stimuli and purposes of another. Yet, it is through separation that they also divide our cities and nations. Through their remarkable utility in the separation of "them" and "us", "inside" and "outside", the concept of the wall has become pervasive. They are just as metaphorical as they are physical; we put up our walls to retreat emotionally from others, we "talk to the wall" when conversation is not reciprocated.

The question that underpins RESOLVE's vision for the future of architecture is simple: what if walls did not separate us, but instead brought us together? To aid in answering this question we have proposed a methodological shift in the various disciplines that constitute and inform architecture, which we call "building by deconstruction". This entails building, creating and synthesising new forms and ideas, through the close examination and deconstruction of old ones. To us, and more importantly to non-architects – like community members, local government groups, activists, developers – this can be difficult to visualise. So to exemplify the approach, we might start by deconstructing the central focus of our project and really try to understand

RESOLVE

RESOLVE are Akil Scafe-Smith, Gameli Ladzekpo, Seth Scafe-Smith, and Vishnu Jayarajan, an interdisciplinary collective who combine architecture, engineering, art and technology in order to address social problems. Previous projects include: the temporary Rebel Space Pavilion in St Matthew's Church Gardens, Brixton for the London Design Festival 2016, which was open 24/7 and made from materials sourced from the immediate neighbourhood. 2017's PassageWay transformed an abandoned space in Brixton Market using over 300 cardboard boxes to create a temporary platform for local creatives and entrepreneurs.

Opposite: The Tree of Life, one of the installations produced by students in the lab.
Image: RESOLVE

or re-understand: What *is* a wall? What else do they do? What are they made of? What *can* they be made of?

Walls can shape

The Fra Mauro Map (see overleaf) is a map of the world that was made by a Camaldolese monk in fifteenth-century Italy. In what's depicted as South East Asia on the map, the landscape is littered with walled cities, between which lie vast swathes of unknowable, impermeable wilderness. Here, in perception at least, walls not only divide the urban from the rural, but demark the effective shape of Late Medieval, Western European imagination.

Walls can be resistance

In the book *Keep Your Eyes on the Wall*, containing responses to the West Bank Barrier wall, Raeda Saadeh's moving photographic portrait, *One Day*, demonstrates how that which resists might become "resistance". The artist is shown with a length of rope attached to a particularly decrepit section of the wall. Poised as though dragging the concrete behemoth, her very presence in, and interaction with, the scene obscures the relationship between *context* and *content*. For the duration of the camera's shutter-speed, resistance is not political struggle against the apparatus of an oppressive regime or the mechanical properties of hardened concrete. Instead, in the grip of Saadeh's yoke, the wall is without power, its purpose co-opted to empower, as a site of resistance.

Walls can make places

London Wall is a familiar sight to anyone who knows the Barbican area in central London. Long past any practical utility, this Ancient Roman vestige exists primarily through its creation of place. The city is no longer contained within its gates but has grown from them, as anyone who has ever experienced the hustle and bustle of Aldgate, Bishopsgate or Moorgate can attest to. Once gates at the edges of the city, they are now at its heart.

The walled city of Kowloon, demolished by the British and Chinese governments in 1994, stood without walls ever since they were broken down to make an airport during the Second World War. Thereafter, the city grew – in typical, albeit slightly augmented, Hong Kong fashion – upwards.

Walls can be made of rooms

Aerial view of the Kowloon Walled City taken in 1989.
Image: Ian Lambot
CC BY-SA 4.0

Its city walls became all the bedrooms, bathrooms, living rooms and kitchens that found themselves at the border between Kowloon and the world beyond.

Unlike many other government-led or UN-sanctioned refugee camps, Dadaab in Kenya, once the largest camp in the world, has no walls, fences or boundaries. Its inhabitants are instead walled in by the war in neighbouring Somalia, hundreds of miles of desert and strict employment restrictions under Kenyan law. In his book *City of Thorns*, which follows the lives of nine refugees in Dadaab, Ben Rawlence writes: "There were no fences around the makeshift city... there was simply nowhere to go."

Walls can be made of nothing

*Walls can be made
from absence*

For the construction of the so-called Great Firewall of China,
no one "sank the first stone into the ground" as Franz
Kafka wrote in his 1917 short story *The Great Wall of
China*. Yet, as in Kafka's short story, it is a wall made of an
abundance of human material: data, or more specifically
the code to filter data. This is a wall that, like walls before
it, surrounds a nation, separates "them" from "us" and yet
it bears no similarity to the material of those walls. This is
a wall made from the absence of information.

People can be walls

Donald Trump's much-trumpeted border wall between
the United States and Mexico may well be the one of most
famous walls in non-existence. Despite not being there,
Trump's wall has worked to insidiously divide opinions
and encapsulate the country's fast increasing divisions. Since
the US presidential election in November 2016, race-related
hate crimes and bias incidents have been reported to have
risen dramatically, with its perpetrators almost unfailingly
all standing behind the same imaginary wall.

*The inhabitable wall /
the wall that inhabits
you*

In the 1990s, in his book *The Borderline Concept: On Private
Madness* the psychoanalyst André Green observed: "You
can be a citizen or you can be stateless, but it is difficult
to imagine being a border". Using data taken from a 2010
consensus in the US city of Detroit, researchers from the
University of Virginia produced a map in which each blue
dot represents one person deemed as white, and each
green dot representing an individual deemed as black. In
this demographic representation the infamous Eight Mile
Road appears akin to any other wall. That, or the bodies
of the mothers, fathers, wives, husbands, children, who
occupy the houses that run along it.

Having explored the conceptual plasticity of walls, our
labs then looked at how the students might materialise

their new understanding of this ubiquitous archetype. After two intense days of designing, project managing and constructing, the participants together devised a 1:1 module that would form a wider configuration of an "inhabitable wall". Containing various amenities aimed at bringing people both to the wall and together around it, the modular assemblage also created a network of multi-level interior spaces – the wall's inhabitable space became a non-hierarchical, Escher-esque maze of chance encounters and random movement.

Importantly, the product of the lab was not the object alone. In deconstructing the processes and perceptions that fortify the divisive notion of walls, it was essential to also reflect upon our own divisions and the divisiveness of our process and perceptions. In light of this, we aimed to carry out the lab less like a workshop and more so as a co-productive endeavour. This was an obvious but integral step in breaking down perhaps the most pervasive division in urban practice: the wall between the practiced-with and the practitioner. ■

Previous spread: The Venetian monk Fra Mauro's map, dated from 1450. This is perhaps the first *modern* world map. It points south because fiftheenth-century compasses were south-pointing. Image: Public Domain

This page: RESOLVE's Akil Scafe-Smith with students during the lab. Image: Vishnu Jay

Safe Spaces

ein FLÄCHENBRAN
Wollt ihr das
den schmeißt die MERKE
Konsorten endlich aus den Pa

Exposing right-wing spaces

**Interview with Stephan Trüby
By George Kafka**

Safe Spaces

Exposing right-wing spaces

Interview with Stephan Trüby by George Kafka

"We realised that many of the so-called private homes of right-wing radicals are not actually private. They are in fact also infrastructural home bases for political movements."

In the period following the political ructions of 2016, increasingly hard lines have been drawn between filter bubbles and spaces on both the Left and the Right. In response to the political pivoting of former-colleagues, the architecture theorist and writer Stephan Trüby has been researching how these tendencies translate into built form. In this interview, he explains his interest in what he terms "right-wing spaces", the subject of his forthcoming book, and reflects on the role architecture plays not only in in their creation and but also their sustainment through being disguised.

Stephan Trüby

Stephan Trüby is a theoretician and professor of architecture and cultural theory at the Munich Technical University. From 2009 to 2014 he ran the postgraduate programme MAS Scenography / Spatial Design at the Zurich University of the Arts and from 2012 to 2014 he was a lecturer in architecture theory at Harvard University's Graduate School of Design. He was also head of research and development for the 2014 Venice Architecture Biennale, directed by Rem Koolhaas.

What led you to begin researching right-wing urban spaces and architecture?

There's a kind of biographical starting point and a theoretical starting point. I'll start with the latter and the question: "what is interesting about architecture?" I would answer by saying that architecture is interesting not because some buildings are nice or work well. For me, the most interesting aspect of architecture is the fact that it is a kind of crossing point where different trajectories – from politics, economics, science, technology and art – come together. Architecture is relevant for the world beyond it because of the meeting of those different agencies. And obviously if you want to be a good architect you need to be competent not only in the fields of technology or art, but also in the fields of economics or politics. Autonomous architecture doesn't exist; architecture is always, at the end, or maybe also at the beginning, a political project. That's the theoretical basis of this work.

The biographical basis is a kind of personal shock. I realised shortly after I completed my PhD with the philosopher

Previous spread: Right-wing demonstration in Chemnitz, protesters march during a rally of right-wing populist movement 'pro Chemnitz' in central Chemnitz, Germany, 07 September 2018.
© EPA-EFE, Franz Fischer

and cultural theorist Peter Sloterdijk that I was part of an intellectual group where right-wing thinking was becoming somehow normalised. The racism of [the German politician] Thilo Sarrazin for example, was often defended. And Marc Jongen, the philosopher and former assistant of Peter Sloterdijk, later became an AfD politician. When I realised this, I started to work against it.

How did these two things – your architectural and political convictions and the recent resurgence of the far right – come together?

Previously I have argued that there's no such thing as "right-wing architecture" or "left-wing architecture", but there is a major distinction between a more regional and a more global approach to what architecture is. Both of these conditions of architecture can either be right-wing or left-wing. Similarly, we can see local or regional approaches to architecture that can again be right wing or left wing. They can be *völkisch* [folkish], but they can also be a kind of local architecture in the form of a leftist project working against an economic or global organisation.

So you don't think there is something like right-wing architecture but that there are right-wing spaces?

Maybe you're aware of the discussion around the LD50 gallery in London.[1] To talk about the architecture of LD50 is probably not interesting. The same applies for the headquarters of Cambridge Analytica. If we look at their building close to Tottenham Court Road station, also in London, we can't establish a link between the ideology of Cambridge Analytica and the office building which they rent. So indeed I would say that architecture and right-wing politics don't come together as right-wing architecture, but actually as right-wing *spaces*.

1 LD50, an east London gallery, was accused of perpetuating an alt-right agenda. The gallery closed in March 2017.

The most extreme and well-known example of *völkisch* approaches to architecture is German national socialism. One of the core political Nazi ideas was *Blut und Boden,* blood and soil. It meant that certain races have their perfect place in a certain landscape.

Can you give an example?

If you travel to some rural areas in Germany, you can come across small villages that were abandoned twenty or twenty-five years ago. In more recent years these same villages have been bought up by neo-Nazis who have started from scratch with a kind of new ethnically homogeneous way of living. They've started to adopt a kind of anti-liberal, anti-urban way of life in these areas. The aesthetics of these settlements are sometimes completely normal, but sometimes also slightly or openly paranoid, with highly articulated boundary condition and high fences and a flag in the middle, with a differentiation made between a peaceful interior and a hostile outside world. Sometimes, these settlements work like camps.

Settlements of right-wing extremists in the United States, such as the KKK or Aryan Nations, are similar, but often more extreme. If you look at the aesthetics of these settlements the you realise that they are always based on the same elements: fences, flags plus architectural typologies which provide communal life easily. Many of these camps copy hippie ways of life from the 1960s and 70s. However, the difference between them is that the right wing idea of communal living is based on the idea of a purity of race or of group and that there is a strong interest in gaining dominance over the outside world.

Are there similar examples in other countries?

By tracing these organisations and people on a map and identifying ownerships etc. we can identify infrastructures – between people, party offices and publishing houses, for example. We can assume links between different groups and speculate also about co-operations.

You mentioned previously that you've visited some of these rural camp sites as part of your research. What does that involve?

That's the dangerous part of the research. Many of the sites I visit are highly secured because they might get attacked by the Antifa. The inhabitants are aware of people looking at their houses and some of them are very quick at calling together a group of neo-Nazis who might follow you there. But I did a couple of trips with friends to different regions, mainly in Germany. We try to identify the houses, the locations, the boundary conditions etc. Not in order to attack these houses but just to think: what does it mean to be there? And you can make a couple of very interesting observations. For example, the numbers of the houses often follow a hidden number code. 18 in German stands for the first and the eighth letter in the alphabet, A and H: Adolf Hitler. You come across many of these. You can also see this with the number plates of the cars.

We try to be careful, especially in areas where we don't know the shortcuts and hidden paths. We don't want to get beaten up, obviously, but we do want to know more about these locations and these sites and these buildings.

In order what to find out exactly?

In order to find out more about what some right-wingers call "meta-politics". It's actually a term born in leftist ideology and is from [Antonio Francesco] Gramsci, the Italian socialist/communist philosopher. Meta-politics means that in order to gain cultural and political hegemony you need to work in a field which is not yet politics: everyday life, media, art and so on. But in my opinion this distinction between private life and public political life doesn't work for right-wing ideologies, because for the people living in these camps, declaring them as territory for an ethnically purified population is a political act already. Through our research we realised that many of the so-called private homes of right-wing radicals are not actually private. They are in fact also infrastructural home bases for political movements. This is why we want to question privacy in many of these homes. By travelling there, we want to find evidence that what is going on there is actually political and just not meta-political.

Considering the conflicts around Confederate Monuments and the Charlottesville Unite the Right March in the US, would you see these as rightist spaces as well?

As in Germany, also in the US the cultural debates about monuments are the first step for right-wing extremists to arrive in the inner-city. This debate about monuments is the first step in a strategy of entering the inner-cities – and the second step would be to establish houses in the inner-city, not just in the countryside. In Germany we have seen a similar debate about monuments through Peter Eisenmann's Memorial to the Murdered Jews of Europe in Berlin. Neo-Nazis and right-wing extremists from the AfD are suggesting that this Holocaust memorial is not, as they say, "atmospheric enough" and not "beautiful enough" to be placed so close to the Brandenburg Gate. They argue for it to be moved to the outside of the city where it would be less prominent. The message is very clear: let's move everything that reminds us of the Holocaust out of the city centre. ■

The Political Church

Heritage as a tool for engagement

By Martin Pohl

The Church of Christ the Saviour in Pristina, was planned as a Serbian Orthodox church during the conflict of the 1990s, when Slobodan Milošević attempted to consolidate Serbian control over the (then) mainly Albanian province of Kosovo.[1] By the time of its construction in the mid-90s, much of this population had been pushed out of the Kosovan capital's city centre.[2] Since then, the church has been neither finished nor destroyed. Its interim state reflects a political condition, symbolising the retreat of the Serbian forces from the city and the fall of the Milošević regime: a temporary state, preserved in architecture. This state, however, can be altered by changing perceptions of the building.

Our ongoing research aims to look beyond the building as an illustration of Serbian nationalism and to instead view it as a readable object in a post-conflict debate about disputed architecture. It asks how we might deal with buildings like this in other post-conflict situations, both locally and globally.

Martin Pohl

Martin Pohl is a German architect and researcher. Educated at the Bauhaus University in Weimar and Waseda University Tokyo he has been the chief-editor of HORIZONTE – *Journal for Architectural Discourse*, an independent publication which has been exhibited worldwide. He has collaborated with Studio Miessen Berlin on the spatial design for the Estonian Pavilion at the 55th Art Biennale in Venice and Sou Fujimoto Architects in Tokyo. He currently works for ROBERTNEUN Architekten in Berlin.

The Political Church is a project by Martin Pohl, Konrad Angermüller, Michael Kraus, Michael Ott and Matthias Schmitt.

1 Interview with Prof. Ass. Dr. Shemsi Krasniqi in Prishtina, February 7, 2014.

2 Denisa Kostovicova, "Kosovo: The Politics of Identity and Space", *Routledge Advances in European Politics 29* (London; New York: Routledge 2005).

Opposite: The Church of Christ the Saviour. Photo: SCHMOTT

This page: Detail of the Church of Christ the Saviour. Photo: SCHMOTT

Inside view. Photo: SCHMOTT

3 Interview with Rozafa Basha in Prishtina, February 9, 2014.

4 Interview with Ass. Prof. Dr. Shemsi Krasniqi in Prishtina, February 7, 2014.

5 Ljubiša Folić, Masterplan for campus Prishtina, *ANALIZA ARHITEKTONSKE FORME*, (Belgrade, 2005).

In 1973, the Albanian architect Bashkin Femiu proposed a new open-plan campus for the University of Pristina.[3] For Albanians, this represented a site for the dissemination of knowledge, not belief.[4] But in 1989 a new masterplan by Serbian architect and urban planner Ljubiša Folić placed a church in a central position, a gesture that opposed the former function of the campus area.[5]

The church's final design, by Serbian architect Spasoje Krunić, was the winning entry to a 1991 competition and one of numerous religious buildings initiated under the Milošević regime. If it had been completed, 1,389 golden crosses would have been engraved into its natural stone façade [6] – 1389 being the year that the Battle of Kosovo took place, which was much mythologised by Serbian nationalists.

6 Interview Spasoje Krunić in Belgrade, February 3, 2014.

Nearly twenty years after the end of the conflict, the church's future is still unclear. For several years, a rancorous dispute over its legal affiliation has been conducted between the Serbian Orthodox Church and the University of Pristina. However, instead of offering a resolution for the future, this ongoing debate seems only to cement the structure's temporary state as permanent. It has in the meantime become a focal point of political demonstrations, a site for critical art installations and even a temporary squat at one point.

In 1999, NATO-led Kosovo Force soldiers erected a barbed wire fence around the church.[7] A uniform 50 metre radius was drawn around Serbian sites after the end

Photo: SCHMOTT

7 Interview Spasoje Krunić in Belgrade, February 3, 2014.

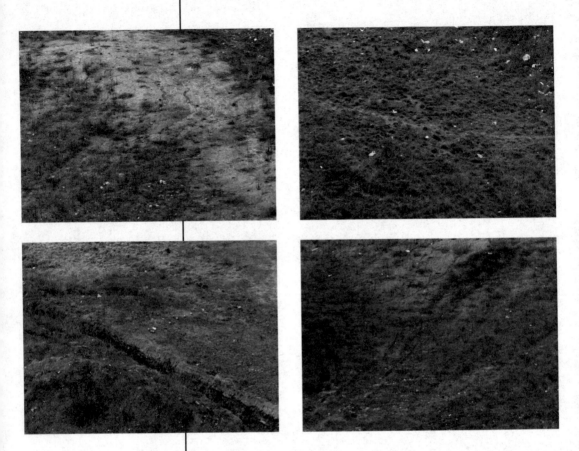

Previous page: The Church and surrounding area. Photo: SCHMOTT

This page: The *50 Meter* photo series. The shards, fragments and passing occupants in and around the ruin, from the pigeons to the scorch marks on the earth, are the disenchanted equivalents of the frescoes and relics of the originally planned architecture. These fragments and imprints could be regard as more important than the actual building itself. Photos: SCHMOTT

of the war to protect them from revenge attacks.[8] In 2016, investigations by forensic experts led them to suspect this contained area to be the site of a mass grave holding missing victims of the war, which has further sensitised the debate about the future of the building.[9] To explore this zone, we engaged in a visual conversation with the photographers SCHMOTT, exploring the site's different spatial manifestations and trying to unravel the multi-layered and conflictual character of the ruin. The resulting *50 Meter* photo series does so without necessarily being bound to established methods and tools of the architectural discipline. Within this perimeter we see a speculative arena for a vital critical debate regarding the ruin's own future as well as the question of collective remembrance.

It is important to state that that we do not necessarily try to develop new architectural solutions and transform contested heritage physically. Instead, we focus on a description of the current state. The aim is to approach this case study, which itself lingers between coexistence and conflict, in an unbiased manner and consciously aware of our position as uninvited outsiders.

Our endeavour to understand the forces that led to this ruined shell relies not upon "taking sides" but instead tracing how existing narratives around the political church are used to serve different opinions. Our ultimate aim is to open up a broader debate: how might interaction with an unwanted, politically-charged and contested building enable a shift towards a more active and continuous form of discourse – legal, architectural and political? ■

8 United Nations Security Council, *Comprehensive Proposal for the Kosovo Status Settlement*, kuvendikosoves. org/common/docs/ Comprehensive%20 Proposal%20.pdf (accessed October 5, 2018)

9 prishtinainsight.com/ search-mass-grave-university-prishtina-campus-begins/ (accessed October 5, 2018)

Progressive Degrowth

The deconstruction of inefficient and exploitative systems in the present is much better than reconstruction after they have failed. Growth can no longer be the ultimate aim. It's time for us to acknowledge and embrace the limits.

Buildings Are Not Enough

Adaptions beyond mere survival

By Tinatin Gurgenidze

Buildings Are Not Enough
Adaptions beyond mere survival

By Tinatin Gurgenidze

"The formation of the spaces is a process that involves the residents and the buildings. Politicians design buildings according to what kind of society they want to establish." *

*Lali,
Gldani resident

Tinatin Gurgenidze

Tinatin Gurgenidze lives
and works in Berlin, her
work concentrates on a
sociological approach towards
architecture and urban space.
She studied architecture and
urban design in Tbilisi and
Barcelona and is currently
working on her PhD thesis
concerning the post-Soviet
mass housing settlement of
Gldani in Tbilisi, Georgia. In
addition to authoring several
publications and lectures,
Tinatin is co-founder of
Tbilisi Architecture Biennial,
which took place for the first
time in 2018.

Previous spread and this page:
Gldani neighbourhood.
Images: Tako Robakidze

October 2018 saw the first edition of the Tbilsi
Architecture Biennial, entitled "Buildings Are
Not Enough". In 2013 the biennial co-founder and
curator Tinatin Gurgenidze started to research
the Georgian capital's Gldani neighbourhood,
interviewing residents and documenting the
ways in which they have adapted the buildings
where they live. Designed as part of a 1970 Soviet
government masterplan, this district on the
urban periphery was intended to house 147,000
inhabitants, from both the city itself and from rural
regions. There is no official figure for how many
people live there today, but unofficial sources
claim it is around 170,000. With no additional
investment coming from the state in response
to this growth, residents began to reconfigure
and adapt their spaces. As this photo essay
shows, Gldani's architecture stands as a record
of these changes, which began immediately after
the collapse of Soviet Union and continue to the
present day.

A room in the Gldani
neighbourhood.
Image: Tako Robakidze

In 1989, towards the end of the Soviet regime, informal extensions to tower blocks were officially sanctioned for a brief period, allowing inhabitants to extend their flats (at their own expense). Lali's family extended their home and built the balcony during the 90s. Even though she thinks the extension was a good decision, she is still afraid it might fall apart because of its unstable construction.

3rd Micro District, 76th Block, 3rd floor, Flat no. 6

"This flat has influenced everything – our careers, motivations, desires. But even though I love this flat, I do think that this space somehow binds us and doesn't allow us to be free."

"The formation of the spaces is a process that involves the residents and the buildings. Politicians design buildings according to what kind of society they want to establish."
Lali, Gldani resident

Gldani neighbourhood.
Image: Tako Robakidze

My Village

Residents constructed their own garages during the late 90s when car theft was a common occurrence. Nowadays, owners rarely park their cars inside them and instead use them for both business and private purposes.

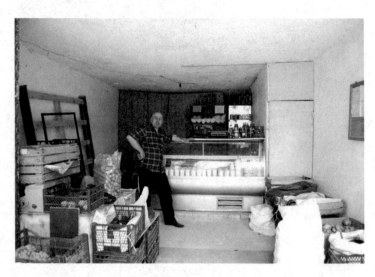

Previous spreads: The Gldani neighbourhood.
Images: Tako Robakidze

This Page: Revaz at his shop garage My Village. Image: Tinatin Gurgenidze

Converted garages in the periphery are the cheapest commercial spaces in Tbilisi. Revaz rents one that houses My Village, a shop selling dairy products and vegetables. Though he has many customers he works every day just to earn money to survive. He hopes to eventually rent a larger, better maintained space.

"I do not have any desire to come here. If this place had been in better condition it would have been different. When I think of going to my ugly working space in a garage I start to feel desperate."

"Nowadays we fight to survive. I would not call this place an income source, but a survival one."

Revaz, My Village shopkeeper

Following conflict between Georgia and Abkhazia in the early 1990s, around 200,000 ethnic Georgian and Abkhazians left their homes. The majority of these internally displaced persons (IDPs) now reside within Georgia in former public administration buildings that were never intended for residential use.

Only a small part of the former Cartographic Institute of Gldani built during the 1970s retains its original use, now 102 IDPs families from Abkhazia call the rest of it home. Tamta spent her whole childhood here and can recall how the hallway would flood whenever it rained through the leaking, damaged roof. She and the other children saw this as an opportunity and turned the flooded hallway into a playground.

The Cartographic Institute

Cartographic Institute of Gldani. Image: Roser Corella

Tamta's parents bought their dwelling some 16 years ago from a private owner and adapted the space to their needs, taking advantage of the high ceiling to create a duplex apartment and even attaching a balcony. Today it is hard to imagine the space ever existed as anything other than a living area.

Urban Gardens

Previous spread: A garage
used as a social space.
Image: Tako Robakidze

This Page: Urban gardens.
Image: Tako Robakidze

Typically, the ground floor areas of the blocks lack light
and privacy, but residents have found a way to compensate
for this disadvantage: almost all ground-floor dwellers
have claimed the land in front of their apartments and
turned them into gardens.

Urban gardening began as a strategy for survival in Tbilisi during the 90s, when residents began cultivating areas to grow their own food. In some areas, like Gldani, this is still a very common practice, with the resulting produce and spices often shared amongst neighbours.* ▪

* A complementary version of this text appears in *Volume 54. On Biennials.* Archis, Amsterdam 2018.

Growing
Realisations

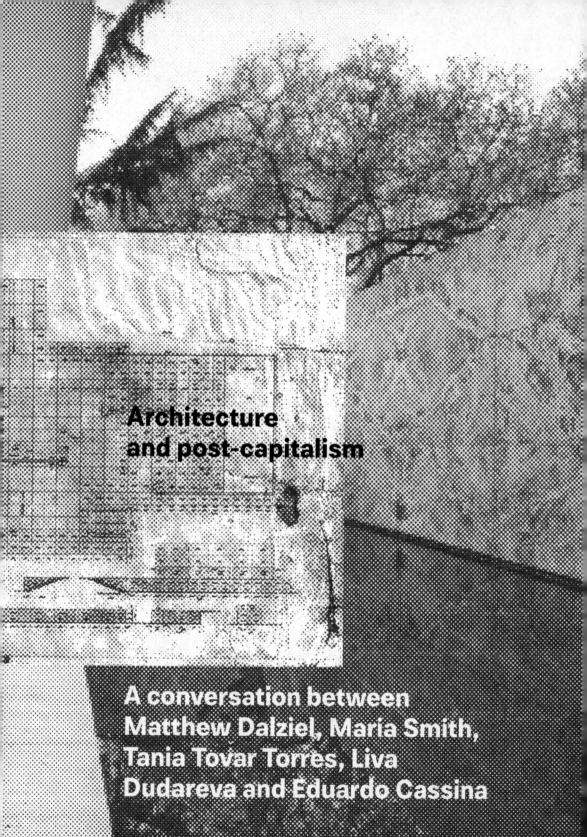

**Architecture
and post-capitalism**

**A conversation between
Matthew Dalziel, Maria Smith,
Tania Tovar Torres, Liva
Dudareva and Eduardo Cassina**

"Degrowth is not about moving in the opposite direction, it's just moving along a different vector."

Growing Realisations
Architecture and post-capitalism

A conversation between Matthew Dalziel, Maria Smith, Tania Tovar Torres, Liva Dudareva and Eduardo Cassina

If the "end of the world" is not an individual event, then perhaps the same logic necessitates that architects think not of how to reconstruct or build anew in the future, but rather the role they could play in the deconstruction of conditions in the present fuelled by unhampered growth, like inequality and accelerating climate change. In this conversation, Matthew Dalziel and Maria Smith, two of the curators of the 2019 Oslo Architecture Triennale, a Future Architecture platform member, discuss how the title and theme of this year's edition "Degrowth" finds parallels in the work of two projects from the FA 2017 open call: METASITU (Eduardo Cassina and Liva Dudareva)'s The Degrowth Institute and Tania Tovar Torres's In Articulo Mortis.

Matthew Dalziel

Matthew Dalziel is an architect and maker working across architecture, education and research. An associate at Interrobang, Matthew now collaborates with clients from artists to airports, previously working for Stirling Prize-winning Haworth Tompkins on housing, theatres and cultural buildings. He has taught in the postgraduate schools of Kingston University and the London School of Architecture.

Matthew Dalziel Let's begin by explaining our own relationships to the term "degrowth".

Maria Smith Our winning proposal for the 2019 Oslo Architecture Triennale focused on exploring the architecture of degrowth, thinking about what architecture practice can do to aid a transition to a post-capitalist economy and considering what practicing architecture is going to be like afterwards. I learned about the term "degrowth" from an architecture student I was critting, who had been researching it whilst working on a project to create a marketplace. They were disillusioned with the idea of creating a space for trade and started to consider what different economic models might look like physically. I immediately became fascinated with the idea and started doing some reading myself.

The call for the Triennale asked entrants to think about the future of architecture in a broad way and I'm generally

Previous spread: In Articulo Mortis image: Barcelona Pavilion Construction Drawing, over Mies van der Rohe, 1929 Barcelona pavilion reconstruction (image: Pete Sieger, 2014).

Maria Smith

Maria Smith is an architect
working across architecture,
engineering, journalism,
education, and events.
She is founding director
of the transdisciplinary
architecture and engineering
practice, Interrobang. She is
also a columnist for the RIBA
Journal; a member of the
RIBA National Awards Panel;
co-founder of Turncoats and
a Design Advocate for the
Mayor of London.

quite obsessed with its overlaps into engineering and
economics. Architects as people are, on the one hand, at the
very frontline of capitalism – helping developers make as
much money as possible from an inflated property market.
But on the on the other, many of us have ideals like that
student: thinking about how space creates or enables
different kinds of social interactions and community.
We have this idealism at university and then we get thrust
into this world that is nothing like what we imagined.

MD My relationship to degrowth is, it's safe to say, a little
bit fraught – I've spent a lot of time trying to convince
my co-curators that we *shouldn't* use the term. Having
lost that battle, I'm very happy to continue examining
it although I have concerns about the misconceptions
that come with degrowth and the potential for it to be
interpreted as a negative term. The research for the
triennale has helped me to recognise that as a process it's
perhaps a consequence of something much bigger that
needs to be addressed. Degrowth is a necessary concept
to propose within the realms of planning and
architectural practice, but if we manage to resolve
larger social problems, then I believe degrowth will
naturally happen. When &beyond first sent through the
information about your two projects, our initial reaction
was: "that's totally not what we mean by degrowth!" But
when we looked closer, we realised that you seem to be
having the same struggles that we are, in that there are
negative and violent connotations to the term but actually
there's an underlying sense of hopefulness to it and it
reflects the sense of a need for consciousness changing.

Tania Tovar Torres: I'm currently setting up a curatorial
platform and exhibition space named Proyector in Mexico
City, which aims to think about how architecture relates

to other disciplines, rather than just supporting its edification. I came in to the topic of degrowth through my In Articulo Mortis project, working more as a writer than an architect even. The project starts with the question of what happens when buildings are no longer there.

Tania Tovar Torres

Tania Tovar Torres is an architect, writer and curator with an interest in architecture narratives. She is founder and director of Proyector, a curatorial platform and exhibition space based in Mexico City devoted to the promotion of architecture research projects. Previously, she worked at the Canadian Centre for Architecture in Montreal, the Arthur Ross Architecture Gallery in New York, the University Museum of Science and Art and the National Council for Educational Development in Mexico City.

Above: In Articulo Mortis image: Cuauhtémoc Tower P.H. 2101 Abandoned Apartment (image: Tania Tovar, 2018) over Cuauhtémoc Tower Tlatelolco Housing Unit (image: Mario Pani, 2018).

Below: In Articulo Mortis image: *The Times*, April 29th 1986 cover over Workers Radiation Check-point at the Chernobyl Plant (image: Michael Forster Rothbart, 2015).

METASITU
(Liva Dudareva
and Eduardo Cassina)

Founded in 2014 by Liva
Dudareva and Eduardo
Cassina, METASITU was born
with the goal of establishing
emancipatory narratives
around the way we inhabit
space, targeting wider
audiences than traditional
architectural and urbanism
circles. METASITU's work
is centred on different
formats of knowledge
exchange and developing
new tools for understanding
the urban condition today
for a queerer tomorrow.
Through the curation of
urbanism festivals, directing
educational programmes,
enabling real estate
transgressions, proposing
workshops, performing
lectures and disseminating
videos, METASITU opens
up new discursive lines, by
involving different actors
into challenging spatial
narratives.

Beyond discussions about physical preservation, we have
to face that fact that we may need let many of them go. So
I started thinking about how to preserve their memory or
essence and to question what it really means to talk about
architecture: could we talk about it in contexts beyond
just the physicality of the object? I started writing stories,
creating constructions of buildings by drawing from
personal accounts, archival records and notes – anything
that I could get my hands on. I was trying then to see
if buildings could live in another format, a process that
starts to challenge what preservation actually means.

I recently spent time in Estonia where these questions
are being discussed a lot in relation to Soviet buildings
that are sitting empty: should they be kept, demolished or
refurbished? And this is all connected to the degrowth of
many different things – of population, of industry and so
on. That's when I began to understand the link between
degrowth as a concept and my own work. I was interested
in one of the quotes from Jill Stoner that &beyond shared
with us about how architecture needs to turn its attention
to "a politics of selectively taking buildings apart". I
wouldn't say that I am actually taking anything apart, but
rather documenting what is being taken apart by other
forces. That's how I start to fit into this conversation.

MD I've been reading some object-oriented ontology
theory (OOO philosophy) in relation to degrowth, which is
really akin to Western philosophy discovering Buddhism
and the idea that all things are connected on an ontological
level. Tim Morton, for example, has written about the
strange collective idea we have of "the away place" – the
notion that when you throw something away, it just goes
to this away place. Human capacity to understand or
engage with death is linked to our lack of imagination

about this place and how it's connected to us. We don't like thinking about our own death and this may contribute to our failures in imagining the death of our objects. we prefer to just let them disappear into this abstraction. But what's happening now is that the away place is starting to colonise the real: global warming is effectively the physical manifestation of the away place. We can't hide from it anymore. We do a similar thing as architects in that we dwell in the excitement of imagining and then realising buildings, before moving on to the next project. But there's often very little reflection on what the life of a building actually is. Another idea Morton has developed is "hyperobjects", which are things that exist in a time-space larger than we can comfortably comprehend. Global warming is a hyperobject but I also think that architecture is a hyperobject in the sense that it's a challenge for us to understand the life cycle of a building outside the abstract.

The inherent problem we have is that we understand that in order to be as sustainable as possible, buildings need to leave no trace and effectively decompose, like everything else in nature. But there is a certain visceral understanding that comes from seeing wear and tear, of seeing the traces of human occupation. How can those two things be reconciled? I'm excited by your project, Tania, because considering the life cycle of buildings is, in a way, similar to how some thinkers are now suggesting we approach global warming: by recognising that one is terminally ill is the beginning of starting to behave differently. Recognising the death of buildings, then, is the beginning of starting to recognise and understand the hyperobject of architecture.

MS METATSITU, what about The DeGrowth Institute project? How do you relate to the term in its title?

> **"We don't like thinking about our own death and this may contribute to our failures in imagining the death of our objects."**

Liva Dudareva We are an artistic duo based between Athens and Kiev and both Eduardo and myself have architectural backgrounds, which is why our work is related to cities, fiction and urban futures. We work to encourage people to look at their surroundings in a different, more emancipatory way, often via knowledge-sharing formats, such as video or installations, workshops and events. The Degrowth Institute is one of our latest endeavours that focuses on shrinking cities in post-Soviet contexts but has parallels beyond these situations, as this is a global phenomenon. Our relationship to the term "degrowth" has been shaped by the fact that degrowth is not a concept but reality in those cities.

DeGrowth Institute workshop at Fondazione Pistoletto. Image: METASITU

The shrinking city in the post-Soviet context the result of a model that was built around one industry. That industry was supplying at least 30 percent of the revenues and essentially sustaining the citizens economically and culturally. Now those factories are slowly shutting down. Given the lack of national subsidies to regenerate these territories or reliance on injections of foreign donations that are often not sustainable, how do you approach cities that will not grow? Because growth is absolutely *not* an option in this context.

Eduardo Cassina A few years ago we went to Ukraine and were asked to make a piece that reacted to the situation in the city of Mariupol, which is in the south-east, right at the border of the conflict in Donetsk. It's a harbour town that is organised around a huge steel factory.

Shrinking needs to be embraced as a positive

Mariupol video essay still. © METASITU

You could feel that the war was very present, but there was also a strong sense of desperation about the lack of jobs and the worsening situation, because the factory was becoming increasingly robotised and production was being outsourced. We went to talk to the city planner of Mariupol and her small team about the future. When we asked her to explain her vision for the city and tell us what we could expect to see if we returned in 2050, she said, "I hope you would see a city with a lot of gardens and skyscrapers and a very busy harbour, something like Hong Kong." This is a city that has been losing people at a rate of ten a day since 1991! This city planner was highly intelligent, yet her answer sounded delusional.

This did not have to do with her personal ambition, but with her job description per se: she needs to plan for *growth*. She had a huge map of the city behind her desk with a colour code for the new areas they were planning to build. But there's no investment. She was spending time and resources thinking how that city could expand whereas if her job description was put differently, she could be using them to think "how are we going to deal with the potential situation, ten years from now when just 100,000 people are left?"

Mariupol video essay still.
© METASITU

That was the trigger for us to think about how we need to shift this paradigm, because almost everyone we spoke to during the trip viewed this shrinkage as the worst thing that could happen. But it could be thought of as positive. We understand the very practical idea that the more people live in one place, the more tax revenues there are but it's also true that it creates a greater demand on the government. Monaco is probably wealthier than

Jakarta – population isn't always the determining factor. It's a question of what the economic model is: Jakarta and Monaco have very different economies.

LD In that way resisting growth is something very positive because it subverts capitalist rhetoric. The way we want to approach the subject of degrowth is by working with locals in some of those shrinking cities, and to encourage them to use it as a tool, to make an empowering statement about being proud of being smaller rather than having to "attract new populations".

MD I think there's something very interesting which has become obvious through this conversation that perhaps wasn't apparent upon first reading your project briefs: there are two very distinct versions of degrowth. There's the kind that we're working with for the Oslo Triennale, degrowth as a thought experiment for globalised society, which is about how to develop limits and a new kind of epistemology that works in places that are growing feverishly as well as in places that are shrinking. Then there's another form, the real, on the ground degrowth that's happening in the places you're describing. I understand Degrowth Institute as helping to deal with the trauma of degrowth. I love your idea of helping people to feel proud and to have a positive relationship with degrowth. Growth is an addiction, so any response to it requires recognising that and then dealing with the trauma of that addiction, in a grounded and reflective way. It doesn't need to be that when a city is shrinking that it feels like there's an absence of growth and therefore there's an absence of substance. There are other forms of substance, like community and ritual and having a sense of place that can rebalance a community of any size.

"Growth is an addiction, so any response to it requires recognising that and then dealing with the trauma of that addiction."

" Resisting growth is something very positive because it subverts capitalist rhetoric."

Previous spread:
Mariupol video essay still.
© METASITU

**" 'Smart decline'
is a form of
terrorism."**

MS There's been an interesting shift on this. Traditionally, environmental concerns have been associated with the political left. But more recently there's been a reframing of environmental concerns through nostalgia. And then the conservatives love it! Suddenly the political right is starting to embrace environmental sustainability and climate issues as a means of harking back to the past.

EC And the nostalgia is often misplaced because the lifespan of a city is larger than the lifespan of a human being. In some of the Soviet, post-industrial centres, there are people alive today who have seen the "peak" of those cities. For them, imagining a time when they were larger is very nostalgic and I can see exactly how that falls into right-wing agendas. The problem is the lack of examples to point to, precedents to show how successful degrowth can be. Many cities in the rust belt in the US have adopted policies of "smart decline", which can involve extremely violent processes like demolishing houses or cutting off communities from public services – as if the term degrowth was already well within our capitalist preconceptions. This is a form of terrorism.

LD This idea of how to degrow in a non-violent way links our project with Tania's. It's about a sensitivity towards a place and the people who have lived there their whole lives. But that also needs to be applied to the shutdown of industries and the feeling of disempowerment that results. A lot of this industrial heritage is not really seen as such, it's seen as a cancer that's destroying everything at this point. Through memory and reflection on this, perhaps what's also needed is the creation of an immaterial heritage. That's not only about nostalgia for the past but also about building something for the future. I see it in the way you described writing and retelling as tools that can help to reconcile the past and carry forward those aspects that are most important.

TTT We're asking people to be ok with the idea of degrowth and having things disappear. But it's something quite unnatural for them – we want to see our things grow old with us. When talking about memory and history, it's not so much about remembering how things were "better" before, but rather finding a way to help us move on to what happens after. The idea of starting to think about buildings and consider their death within our planning is an important one, but at the same time there are so many things that have already been built, with no thought given to their demise. Perhaps introducing a step within the cycle where we acknowledge not just their death but how to preserve their history could be helpful. Maybe something similar to the Mexican Day of the Dead: a rite of passage, crossing a threshold between something disappearing and the acceptance of that. It's one thing for those who are involved in city planning to understand the need for degrowth, but it is much more difficult for the wider community to engage with that kind of thinking.

MS I think it's about humility. We need to recognise that any piece of material that we use to create some edifice for some period of time is not *us*. We shouldn't think that we can superimpose our will onto something and that by creating this magnificent thing that will outlive us we can live forever through architecture. Instead it's about a negotiation between our needs at a particular moment and the material, be it bricks or wood, whatever. These materials have their own agency and intent – we're just borrowing and collaborating with them.

> **"We need to recognise that any piece of material that we use to create some edifice for some period of time is not 'us'."**

"If we're going to live sustainably on Earth, then we need to very actively change the way we think about creating buildings."

What you were saying about degrowth, Tania is connected to the circular economy: thinking not of a linear path, where you just put waste in the away place, but instead view everything as cyclical. If we're going to live sustainably on Earth, then we need to very actively change the way we think about creating buildings – the way we create anything – according to these circular economy principles, whereby there is no such thing as waste. Everything that you produce has to be an input to another process, whatever that process may be. We have to create every building knowing that it can be taken apart and that its constituent parts can become part of something else in the future.

EC Degrowth is not about moving in the opposite direction, it's just moving along a different vector. I don't think it's so much about reversing processes as it's about challenging the linearity that is projected upon those processes.

MD That's why it's so important that any discussion around degrowth concerns changing our thoughts and our actions rather than having a "plan". If we start thinking about making new buildings differently, that's already summoning this tabula rasa idea, saying that "from *today* onwards, everything's going to be different". But yesterday's buildings are an externality to this solution. Whereas if you think and react in a degrowth fashion, then all of the existing built environment becomes part of it too.

We've been very careful in our work to not speak about the literal deconstruction of buildings or non-building. One of the first things we encountered during our first interview for the Triennale was the assumption that that's what we meant. We were asked: "does degrowth mean not building any more buildings?" We answered "no", that as practicing architects, we are interested in the practice of architecture and that degrowth is actually about thinking differently about how we make and care for things. What we need to address, as we have started to do through this conversation, is the difference between the thought experiment of Western thriving growth and changing the way it operates, and how places beyond the West, which aspire to that kind of growth, can find a different way of being. There isn't necessarily a singular solution. ∎

Inter-
dependent
Individuality

The technologies of the digital age are not inherently problematic. They are tools that can be used for oppression, but also empowerment. We can recode and redistribute our technological intelligence into technological agency.

Air Revert

**An architectural toolkit
for mitigating indoor pollution**

By Skrei

When we submitted the Air Revert project to the Future
Architecture platform's call for ideas, we were busy
designing a building made out of earth for a young Chinese
entrepreneur who had little understanding of building
construction but a good intuition for business. At one meeting
we were explaining to him the benefits of earth construction,
particularly in terms of thermal regulation, when he suddenly
stared at me and asked whether plasters made from earth
can purify the air. It was a good question. We knew that
the Ancient Romans used to purify air with clay filters,
but we could not account for why ancient air filtering
technologies are totally absent in contemporary buildings.

Indoor air pollution is a major killer in Asia, therefore air
purification systems are a lucrative business. In China, for
instance, extreme levels of air pollution mean that windows
in new buildings cannot be opened, so all ventilation
depends on centralised inbuilt systems. Over time, this
machinery gradually fails due to maintenance issues and
residents can be subjected to asphyxiation inside their own
homes. According to the World Health Organisation, this
accounts for some 3.8 million deaths a year. [1]

This is not just an urban problem. Winds can carry
poisonous ultrafine particles thousands of kilometres from
the source of pollution. Air currents passing industrial
coal plants in Ukraine, for example, travel as far as natural
reserves in Slovenia or the Adriatic coast of Italy. Scientists
are only just starting to understand the impact of these
tiny particles and their migration. They are by far the
hardest particles to measure and mitigate and are the most
dangerous to human health.

The easiest way to control particulate matter (PM)
pollution would be to ban diesel cars and the use of coal,

Skrei

Skrei is a project design,
construction and artistic
production workshop
initiated by Francisco
Fonseca and Pedro Jervell
in Porto, Portugal. It brings
together various construction
professionals in an integrated
professional practice.
Their aim is to challenge
the traditional role of
architecture by creating new
ways of designing, new ways
of building and models for
a more equitable, healthier
and responsive environment.

[1] who.int/airpollution/en/
(accessed October 5, 2018)

Opposite: enclosed clay
pipe that works as an air
purifying system
Image: Skrei

but could architecture also help deal with the problem? We think it should be able to do so, there are plenty of effective individual systems based on both high and low technologies available. The difficult part is that air pollution, including that from mould and toxins, varies a lot, so an integrated system with a range of capacities would be required. However, despite humankind's vast knowledge of traditional air purification systems, there are no common solutions, particularly when it comes to integrative systems that bring together many traditional, lower-tech technologies. Air Revert explores this technological niche by performing empirical tests on the interconnection of low-tech systems in order to answer a problem that high-tech doesn't seem able or willing to tackle. It combines simple indoor materials, air convection systems and a few climate control devices. It could be used in hospitals, schools and dwellings located in highly polluted areas. The system is scalable and likely to reach patenting at a later stage.

How Air Revert works

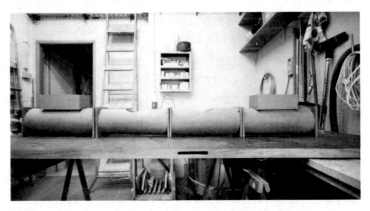

Enclosed Filtering Chambers.
Image: Skrei

There are three main models we are working with, all quite simple. The Enclosed Filtering Chambers involve the connection of different low-tech air filtering systems, each of which is built within its own chamber. Each chamber contains short segments of terracotta pipes and ends in

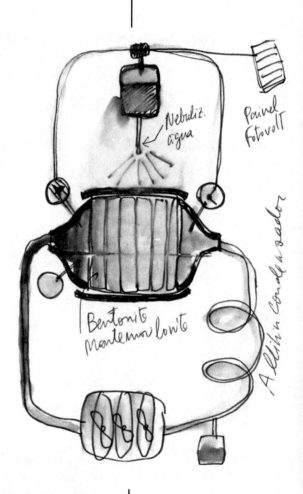

an electric vent, which is in turn connected to the next filtering chamber and ensures the air flows through the system. This modular air conductor brings together the benefits of different filtering systems, from bentonite clay to activated coal, plant roots, oil nebulisers, diffusers, pressure chambers and filters, each of which helps filter a specific kind of air pollution.

The Enclosed Filtering Pipe is an enclosed clay pipe that works as an air purifying system. Certain kinds of clay have filtering capacities. For example, bentonite clay mixed with activated coal acts as a filtering material when it is

Initial concept/ speculative sketch for the plaster cooling system. Image: Skrei

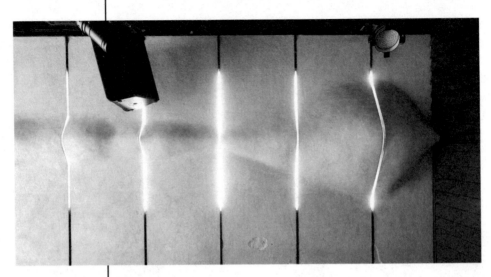

Enclosed clay pipe that works
as an air purifying system.
Image: Skrei

kept sufficiently moist and polluted air brushes against the
damp clay surface. The model consists of a single irregular
clay shaft with alternating wide and narrow sections that
create pressure differences as air is blown through the
pipe. These pressure differences create turbulence inside
the pipe so that polluted air is forced against its damp
interior surface.

Exposed Filtering Surface.
Image: Skrei

Finally, the Exposed Filtering Surface works in the same
way as the enclosed filtering pipe but instead of a pipe you

have an entire surface, such as a wall or ceiling, which filters air when it is blown against its purifying surface. In this system the ceiling is covered with a clay plaster. Clay plaster needs a certain humidity level in order to act as a purifying element. The surface has a number of vents and a sprinkler system that keeps the plaster moist, allowing it to act as a retainer for purifying agents such as oils and activated carbon. The system also regulates indoor humidity, especially in highly-heated spaces where the air tends to get extremely dry.

Air Revert is still in its early stages. Step one, researching ancient and low-tech systems and step two, empirically testing these systems to ascertain practical limitation with models, are complete. The next stage is to find technical and research partners, such as universities and research institutions, in order to develop a testing method for these models. ■

Institute for Autonomous Urbanism

未加工
工坊

Hacking
infrastructure
in Shenzhen

By Jason Hilgefort

I grew up in a small town in Ohio in the US, a very rural place, so for me technology was a really important tool to connect with the outside world. Later, working as an urban planner with my partner Merve Bedir, our office Land + Civilization Compositions (LCC), has undertaken projects in the Netherlands, Nairobi and Shenzhen in which we dreamed up ideas of how the relationship between technology, infrastructure and urban and rural environments could go forward. Our proposal for an Institute for Autonomous Urbanism presents a series of perspectives, proposals and questions on urbanity and rurality and their relationships with infrastructure and technology.

Around the Chinese city of Shenzhen there are villages servicing one of the world's biggest e-commerce websites called Taobao. These are rural places with cheap, skilled labour who have organised themselves to produce low-priced objects for online sale. A lot of these small villages were once poor but have now become factories containing millionaires and billionaires. We wanted to understand and study this, so we looked at some of the successful examples, not just in terms of their urban form, but also the economic and social models of how these projects were funded. Following this, we put together some workshops in Xinguang in Guangzhou, Guangdong where there are some semi-abandoned villages slowly being encroached upon by the city of Shenzhen. We asked what these villages can do to take advantage of the opportunities this might bring whilst still embracing their own culture. We also looked at examples of small technologies that are available in the region, such as drones and high-end satellite imagery, considering how they could transform communities via economic opportunities for the residents and what this could mean for the urban planning of the area.

Jason Hilgefort

Jason Hilgefort studied at the University of British Columbia and the University of Cincinnati. He has worked with Peter Calthorpe, Rahul Mehrotra, Maxwan and ZUS. He won Europan 11 in Vienna and founded Land+Civilization Compositions, a Rotterdam/ Hong Kong based studio. He was a subcurator in the Shenzhen/HK Urban/Arch Biennale and co-director of its learning platform. Currently, he is the International Director of FUTURE+Aformal Academy.

Technology and the rural

Opposite: Plastic injection molded parts in Guangyang Molds Products Co, Shenzhen. Image: Mitch Altman CC BY-SA 2.0

Hacking infrastructure

Since the success of the High Line in New York, more and more people have become aware of the role of infrastructure, what it means in their lives and have started adapting it to their own environments. "Hacking infrastructure" is about how people reinterpret spaces.

Burnside Skatepark under the Burnside Bridge (Portland, Oregon). Image: Kyle Burris CC BY-SA 2.5

Different communities have different approaches and different solutions. In the US, for example, you will often find skateparks in the spaces below highways. But in other places, where there is a highway running through informal settlements, the space underneath bridges becomes an informal retail space or a space to live. Infrastructure also does not necessarily mean physical spaces: in the West there is also a lot of hype around how "all the robots are going to take our jobs", but many people we talked to in Shenzhen, for example, don't agree with that at all. They talk in terms of "co-bots", and their attitude towards technological advances in this area is one of collaboration and transition. The Institute for Autonomous Urbanism is about thinking how we can visualise and communicate such ideas to architects and to a broader public using installations, film, maps and flows, and preparing for how and when the autonomous city comes into our lives.

For us, autonomous urbanism takes this a step further
to consider that maybe we don't need infrastructure to
come from the government, which potentially allows
for a completely different way of thinking about how
communities work and how they are funded. If they don't
need to build streets, or sewers, or power grids, what
is the role of government and how do we deal with the
public spaces between our buildings? Are they even public?
What do we do if we're making a city for robots? What does
that look like?

Autonomous urbanism

In 1900, before the arrival of the elevator and the car,
no one saw what was coming in terms of all the small
technologies that were about to change the world's cities.
We need to start getting ahead of this and think about
how these cities can be visualised and how our rural
places will change as these new technologies completely
alter everything we have become accustomed to. ■

Furniture designer Fernando
Abellanas's studio, built
beneath the overpass of
a busy traffic bridge in
Valencia, Spain. Image: Jose
Manuel Pedrajas

S'lowtecture

Concept for a modular, algorithmic housing structure

By Tomasz Broma

Let's imagine that architectural space is a huge, interactive game board. And we, as users of this space, are active players who may directly and dynamically transform the game board with different types of resources and raw materials. These can be processed and crafted with tools gathered in the inventory according to our individual skills, requirements, financial capability and the style and pace of our lives. This is how s'lowtecture works. It is a process of creating a housing structure in which users can freely decide the arrangement of their own houses and common public space. This is achieved via a three-dimensional cellular automaton algorithm that generates various different housing units and places them within the structure.

Tomasz Broma

Tomasz Broma is an architect based in Wrocław, Poland who holds a masters degree from Wrocław University of Science and Technology (WUST). In 2016, he was the winner of a Young Talent Architecture Award from the Fundació Mies van der Rohe. He continues his research as a PhD candidate at WUST exploring different aspects of low-tech strategies.

Opposite: The s'lowtecture housing structure prototype. Image: Tomasz Broma

This page: House unit with fabric materials. Image: Tomasz Broma

The concept of s'lowtecure is based on five pillars: the hypothesis of atavistic space assuming that our spatial preferences were formed during the process of biological and cultural evolution, a self-organised and shared society, low-tech, slow movement, and participatory architecture. The resulting s'lowtecure is experimental, spontaneous and vital; flexible, open-minded and creative; democratic, inclusive and egalitarian; cooperative and socially sensitive; ingrained in place, traditions and craft.

Rules

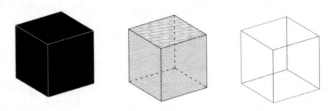

The s'lowtecture algorithm divides space into a matrix of cubic cells. Each may be assigned one of three states: a built-up cell, an empty cell or a garden cell. Built-up cells serve as a housing space, garden cells complete housing units and the empty ones provide gaps between houses filled with semi-private spaces that allow encounters between neighbours. In these spaces community facilities like laundries, workshops or small urban farms can also be set up.

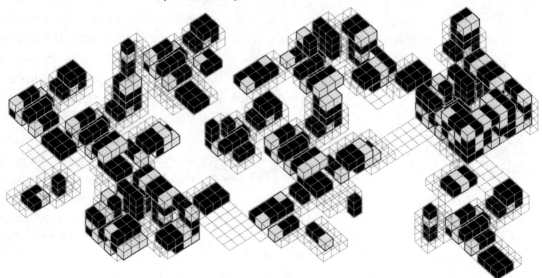

The various states of the cells affect each other. Relations between them are regulated by the algorithm. Its rules are based on the analysis of the surrounding neighbourhood and allows the generation of complex, dynamically adaptable and emergent structures. Within them are typologically diverse housing units – from two-celled, single-person micro-units to multicellular and multi-level houses. The algorithm efficiently accommodates units into the cellular structure but gives inhabitants as much independence as possible when building their homes. Whilst preserving this autonomy, the game determines the most rational use of the available space, guaranteeing appropriate distances between housing units to provide access to sunlight, facilitate communication and connect with infrastructure. It also prevents spatial blockages and conflicts. A vibrant and flexible housing structure is created, comprising housing units suited to inhabitants' needs, with individual gardens and community space.

The s'lowtecture housing structure prototype would be installed above a FabLab where inhabitants use tools to prepare the materials required to build their houses. These are easily available and local, natural or recyclable materials that do not require long-distance transportation or energy-intensive manufacturing processes. Instead, simple, open-source technologies are used to create each of the building systems described in a step-by-step guide. Construction experiments and experiences are collected into an ever-expanding ideas pool to serve future inhabitants. By committing their own time and energy towards construction, inhabitants' costs are reduced, they can adapt or rebuild the house according to changing needs and, above all, have a sense of belonging and independence. ■

DIY prototype

Power to the Peer

A conversation about the distribution of energy and housing via blockchain-based platforms

Interview with DOMA (Maksym Rokmaniko and Francesco Sebregondi) and Phi (Aliaksandra Smirnova)
By George Kafka and Fiona Shipwright

Power to the Peer

A conversation about the distribution of energy and housing via blockchain-based platforms

Interview with DOMA (Maksym Rokmaniko and Francesco Sebregondi) and Phi (Aliaksandra "Sasha" Smirnova) By George Kafka and Fiona Shipwright

"Blockchain can ideologically and technologically enhance architectural practice and finally bring to life ideas about architecture as a complex system of relationships and connections, rather than bricks and stones."

The growing popularity of blockchain systems for organising and distributing information is creating new, network-based architectures. Exploring the possibilities of blockchain-based systems for the built environment are two speculative projects submitted to the Future Architecture platform: DOMA, an affordable housing platform, and Phi, a clean energy platform. In this conversation, conducted via Slack, &beyond's Fiona Shipwright and George Kafka discuss the potential of these projects to create socially sustainable and equitably distributed solutions to our basic domestic needs.

Phi

Aliaksandra Smirnova is an urbanist and a co-founder of Phi. Phi is an international collective working at the intersection of peer-to-peer technologies, energy futures, and speculative design. Their projects imagine new ownership models to enable sustainable futures and reform how value is recognised and socialised. Phi is Calum Bowden, Cory Levinson, Aliaksandra Smirnova, Artem Stepanov, and Aiwen Yin.

George Kafka [6:04 PM]
joined #phi-and-doma.

George Kafka [10:30 AM]
Morning all!
Have we got everyone here? Phi...Doma...Fiona?
:neutral_face:

maksy [10:35 AM]
joined #phi-and-doma by invitation from George
Kafka, along with 3 others.

Fiona Shipwright [10:35 AM]
Good morning!

Sasha [10:36 AM]
Hi! Phi is here
:slightly_smiling_face:

FSBRG [10:36 AM]
Hi
I'm around too

Previous spread: Network.
Image: Phi

George Kafka [10:37 AM]
ok super
To start off, perhaps it would be best for each
of you to briefly introduce yourselves and let
us all know where you're joining from. I'll
start - I'm George, I'm editing Archifutures
5 with &beyond and I'm currently in sunny
London...

Fiona Shipwright [10:38 AM]
I'm Fiona, I'm also editing Archifutures 5 with
&beyond and I'm in slightly overcast Berlin

FSBRG [10:40 AM]
Hey I'm Francesco, from DOMA, and I'm based
in Paris.

Sasha [10:40 AM]
I'm Aliaksandra (Sasha), I'm a co-founder
of the project Phi and I'm talking from Moscow
with a perfect temperature today.

maksy [10:40 AM]
I am Maksym, from DOMA, joining from Kyiv.

George Kafka [10:42 AM]
Thanks again all for joining. Please feel free
to take as long as you need to answer - one
of the aims of doing this in Slack is to allow
a bit of thinking time

George Kafka [10:42 AM]
For this issue we are exploring the theme
of "apocalypse" in which we are trying to
interrogate what that word means and what
implications it has for the future
of architecture.

Fiona Shipwright [10:45 AM]
I would also add to that we're interested in
the idea of the apocalypse as a long term
process, not just a binary "before/after"
event.

FSBRG [10:46 AM]
It's interesting because, as far as DOMA
is concerned, we actually try to stay away from
notions of resilience and survival in times of
impending crisis as we think these notions tend
to fuel the crisis rather than solving it,
so in the face of real urgencies, we're trying
to deploy a long-term strategy.

George Kafka [10:47 AM]
Perhaps to start could you explain a little bit
about the contexts in which you are working?
For example, DOMA, why did you choose to
address housing issues where you are? And Phi,
was there a particular situation that inspired
your focus on energy systems?

FSBRG [10:49 AM]
Well I think wherever you are today in our
urban world, you can't really escape the
so-called housing crisis. We see it as a
structural feature of the twenty-first century
city.

Sasha [10:52 AM]
First, I would like to highlight again the idea
that Fiona mentioned, that you're interested
in processes and strategy rather than points
in time. I think it's very important for Phi.
Regarding the initial ideas and concepts that
are behind Phi, I think we're interested and
imagining how a world that is no longer based
on scarcity but on abundance could look like.
From our point of view this transition starts
with energy.

FSBRG [10:53 AM]
DOMA set out to imagine not so much a way out
of this crisis, but a way across it. Using the
financialisation of housing to achieve opposite
goals to its current ones, playing the market
against the market, recognising the widening
urban inequality gap as our site
of intervention.

DOMA

Maksym Rokmaniko and
Francesco Sebregondi are
architects and co-founders
of DOMA. DOMA is a
blockchain-based, shared
ownership platform for
equitable housing. Bridging
the great divide between
renting and home ownership,
DOMA leverages the
principles of the new token
economy to make urban
property accessible to all.

Phi and DOMA were both initially conceived at the same time and in the same context – The New Normal programme at the Strelka Institute in Moscow – so we have a lot in common in our ways of thinking and tackling the urgencies of our urban future.

We're cousins basically.

Sasha [10:56 AM]
So, we're asking what the social and economic values of such a world would be. How the aforementioned abundance of resources (energy) will transform social relationships and reconfigure distribution of power.

George Kafka [10:58 AM]
The other connection that is quite obvious is how both of your projects utilise blockchain technology – was that something you both explored at Strelka? Can you explain why that technology might be important for the future of architecture?

Sasha [10:58 AM]
Yes, actually DOMA and Phi were initially going to be same project. The first idea was that Phi would be an infrastructure and DOMA could implement their system.

FSBRG [11:01 AM]
To your question @George Kafka. I guess we're not lacking grand narratives about the revolutionary potential of blockchain technology, the use cases and impact of which could extend to every domain of our contemporary life. In order to speak about its impact on architecture, I think one needs to think about architecture in an expanded sense – not only the architecture of buildings, but of systems of relations.

In that sense, the question for me is the other way around: what can architecture do for blockchain? I think architectural thinking has a big role to play in negotiating the right "blockchain revolution" ahead.

Sasha [11:04 AM]
Talking about Phi, we can say that blockchain has two main functions in our project: techno-economic and social. The first one is quite straightforward, we use blockchain to store the information about energy consumption on a public ledger that will allow us to generate tokens with a certain value. Those tokens will have a social function that will create an incentive for people to transition from fossil fuels to clean energy sources.

George Kafka [11:05 AM]
As part of the process of making this book, &beyond are also considering the radical acts of *hope* and *trust* in the face of apocalypse (environmental, social, political catastrophe) - following on from your comment about "systems of relations" @FSBRG, do you see these notions as part of your projects? Or to put it another way, what might be the social consequences of Phi and DOMA, beyond their primary functions relating to housing and energy?

FSBRG [11:11 AM]
Perhaps a very real aspect of the "apocalypse" is our current, globally pervasive crisis of hope and confidence towards the future. I think DOMA is driven by a will to challenge that. It's an experiment that tries to use blockchain technology in order to assemble a new collective agency. One that is capable of scaling up, in order to face the forces of a rigged housing market, which condemns the large majority of urban dwellers to a lifetime of rent, of long-term exploitation and alienation. So it's about trying to prove that it's actually not impossible to regain a degree of hope in our urban condition, and reconfigure

some of its key logics so that it can become
more inclusive and more sustainable in the
long run.

Sasha [11:15 AM]
I think that those notions are very important
for Phi since it was conceived as an answer to
the climate change issue and the incapability
of central authorities and governments to deal
with it.

FSBRG [11:16 AM]
It sounds naive, but I think we almost need
some naivety today. There are things that
we can change, right now. The technology
to support it is mature. Perhaps it's the
collective will that isn't.

maksy [11:19 AM]
Yes, but I think people are also more and
more aware that what we are facing is not a
crisis of production, in terms of housing –
it is a crisis of distribution. And I think,
politically, there is a demand for movements
addressing that.

Sasha [11:20 AM]
By proposing a collectively-owned energy
system Phi aims not only to secure clean
energy but also be a kind of an educational
tool for people to understand how the energy
system works. We hope that it will create an
understanding of collective responsibility for
rising temperatures and melting ice.

George Kafka [11:21 AM]
I think there's something really interesting in
the idea of how p2p networks might facilitate
a form of community underpinned by a digital
infrastructure, as opposed to a physical one.
That, to me, is where the hope lies in these
projects, would you agree?

Fiona Shipwright [11:22 AM]
I also wanted to pick up on what you just said
Sasha about being an educational too. What both
these systems do is make visible materials and
process flows. Although some may feel blockchain
is complicated or "difficult", it makes those
flows much more visible than, say, "traditional"
modes of architecture production.

Sasha [11:25 AM]
Exactly. I think blockchain can ideologically
and technologically enhance architectural
practice and finally bring to life ideas
about architecture as a complex system of
relationships and connections, rather than
bricks and stones.

FSBRG [11:32 AM]
I guess both our projects acknowledge that
our contemporary experience of a "community"
is an increasingly mediated one and that,
when it comes to acting as a community, the
question of designing the medium by which such
communities can exist today becomes crucial.
Both our projects - @Sasha correct me if I'm
wrong! - revolve around exploring the potential
of blockchain to achieve coordination and
consensus among a mass of distributed users
at scale. The problem of scale is critical
here because of the wicked problems we are
respectively trying to address - the global
housing crisis for DOMA, climate change for
Phi. With DOMA, one of the central question
for us is: what is the minimal infrastructure
we can design to allow vast amounts of urban
dwellers to act as a single community of
interest?

Sasha [11:34 AM]
Following up on Fiona's comment, the central
point of Phi is the user. Basically, Phi is an
interface to complex systems (such as energy
or blockchain) that treats users equally.

That means that Phi aims to translate such
systems into a "human" language without hiding
information about how these systems actually
work. And we want to achieve this by giving the
user decision-making power.

Sasha [11:45 AM]
The scaling issue is something we are
constantly dealing with in our project. Phi
was initially thought of as a "global energy
network empowered by blockchain technology".
But at the moment of actual implementation we
obviously have to narrow our ambitions and
face up to real life factors. So we developed
strategies to build a minimum unit for a
scalable system that didn't lose touch with
our initial philosophy, and could still co-
exist with the current socio-political climate.
It's not an easy task, but bringing our ideas
from a speculative world into the real one is
definitely worth the effort.

George Kafka [11:47 AM]
So what is the future for Phi and DOMA? How
do you plan to take them from the speculative
to the real? When will I be able to live in a
DOMA property or source my energy from the Phi
system?

Sasha [11:53 AM]
We're currently working on the implementation
of Phi. We're interested in building a working
prototype, a sort of a test-case at the
urban scale, that will allow us to showcase
our system. We are also in conversation with
several companies and start-ups that could
provide us with the hardware (e.g. batteries
and solar panels) and we're working on a
software focusing on UX (user experience) and
UI (user interface) that will help people to
manage decentralised renewable sources.

maksy [11:54 AM]
We are convinced that the level of crisis and
the level of urgency in which we find ourselves
today in relation to the housing crisis,
demands long-term, bold, ambitious visions,
rather than emergency solutions and piecemeal
actions. We are planning an experiment aimed at
testing our core strategies: crowd-buying of
property and equity distribution.

Sasha [11:59 AM]
I hope that there will be more news and
developments soon

George Kafka [11:59 AM]
That seems like a good place to end the
conversation. Thanks again for your time
and thoughts this morning, it's been super
interesting and I'm excited to now work out
a way to translate this conversation onto a
printed book!

Fiona Shipwright [12:00 PM]
Thank you very much everyone for the really
interesting thoughts to continue thinking on.

George Kafka [12:03 PM]
:wave: